DAVID'S HARP

Returning Harmony to Conflicted Congregations

BILL KEMP

DISCIPLESHIP RESOURCES

P O BOX 340003 • NASHVILLE, TN 37203-0003
www.discipleshipresources.org

Cover design by Christa Schoenbrodt

ISBN 13: 978-0-88177-530-3

Library of Congress Control Number: 2008924132

Contents

Preface: Therapeutic Harps

David had a magic harp. Well, maybe not magic in the way we tend to think of magic. Whenever Saul went nuts, David played his harp and Saul calmed down. When our congregation goes nuts, we church leaders want that magic harp. If it came up for auction on eBay, we would bid half the money in the sacred memorial fund to buy the thing. But reading a little further into the story, we see that David's harp was only a temporary bandage for Saul's mania. During one manic fit, Saul picked up his spear and tried pinning his therapist to the wall (I Samuel 18:10-11). Temporary fixes do not work in the end.

Page after page of the Bible reveals that conflict is a constant companion of God's people. Jesus does not mitigate the presence of conflict when he teaches his disciples the way of peace. The early church seems to have had as much difficulty with internal friction as it had with the persecution of the church from the outside. Even when the mission is clear, the Spirit palpably present, and the pastoral leadership of Peter and Paul, we see in the New Testament that early Christian fellowships faced contention and conflict, a condition that continues to this day.

This book focuses on conflict and what I label insanity (or bizarre or irrational behavior). First this note: I'm not using insanity in the clinical sense. Sometimes I use it to refer to those times when we keep doing the same thing over and over and over again, but expecting different results. Sometimes I use it to refer to times when someone stomps on

our last nerve. Sometimes the word refers to behavior that may be mali-
cious or hurtful. Sometimes the word embraces behaviors that
demonstrate a lack of health.

Laity and clergy need to learn a few notes from David's harp to calm
the emotional tsunamis that regularly wash through even the best of
churches. We need to go beyond merely ducking the spears that people
throw at us simply because we hold a position of leadership or because
we have inadvertently uncovered or stepped into a longstanding mess left
untouched for years. We need to develop practical and positive tech-
niques for managing congregational anxiety. We also need to understand
and limit the power of those individuals who, sometimes because of
unresolved emotional issues, seed congregations with chaos and plant
rumors in the crowd. We need to learn how to focus on intentional
peacemaking. When a church deals with its conflicts and divisions with
integrity and its leaders practice compassion towards those who dissent
in all ways, the church offers a profound model for facing and healing
the world's conflicts. Every social setting has its insanity. Nations war
with nations, communities perpetuate classism and racism, and civic
organizations routinely become uncivil. As it seeks to be relevant, the
church must be transparent about its experiences of darkness and about
the healing we have experienced in Christ.

David's Harp provides a small toolbox for conflict resolution. I am
convinced, however, that the best tools can become worse than ineffective; they are dangerous when applied without a sense of perspective.
When we use the latest gift of pop-psychology to dismiss the actions of
those with whom we disagree or whose behavior creates conflict, we may
inadvertently fail to treat a brother or sister in Christ as a human being.
Once headed down this road of seeing others, not as persons like ourselves, but as "that codependent" or that "compulsive neurotic," we
become another part of the problem which needing healing. Used
unwisely, even the best conflict-resolution tools may deepen the alien-
ation people feel from one another and may make the conflict
irreparable. One of my teachers quoted with fondness a folk aphorism:
"To the person with a hammer, every problem looks like a nail." To the

church leader equipped with the latest management technique, every conflict looks like a simple matter of fixing one or two people. Instead of providing a dozen ways to get people to "yes" or agreement, *David's Harp* offers a new way of seeing the congregation as a total system. When we managed congregational systems well, we ground normal policies in love and reach out in ministry and mission. When we honor the relational fabric of a congregation, churches grow and capture the energy inherent in diversity of opinions.

I believe conflict is a valuable thing in the church. That may not make much sense now, but it should become clear as you read this book. I am convinced that God's Spirit does not wish for any congregation to flounder in controversy until all hands escape or are lost. Christ's mission is too important for any church, using the image of church as the ship of faith, to drop its anchor in the safe harbor of consensus. An engaged church, seeking ways to witness to Christ in its locale, will routinely risk ill winds in order to achieve new goals. How to remain courageous in the midst of conflict's gales is the primary leadership lesson that this book offers to both clergy and laity.

May the God of peace, known in the shalom of Jesus Christ, bless us with the discernment to see grace ever in our midst.

Bill Kemp
Advent 2007

Introduction: Conflict and Incompetence

*Never attribute to malevolence that which
is merely due to incompetence.*

Arthur C. Clarke (*3001: The Final Odyssey*), 187.

Arthur C. Clarke's simple words offer a great wisdom. I do not believe that the devil seeds congregations with conflict in an attempt to foil God's glory. I do not find it helpful to blame conflict on other people, whether clergy or laity, who may commandeer or hijack the church for their own purposes. My experience as an intentional interim pastor confirms Arthur Clarke's wisdom: Most conflict happens because of some form of incompetence.

As a church leader who has been responsible for more than my share of conflicts, I write about this conflict-incompetence connection with a sense of humility and an awareness of my own mistakes. If we congregational leaders fail to monitor and maintain the church's decision-making process, then it is inevitable that someone or something will derail that process. If we are blind to the family systems that underlie the relationships of our fellowship, then explosive conflict that erupts over who is allowed to do what and with whom will blindside us.

In general, if we fail to develop accountability at each level of our organization, those who serve as pastors and staff will spend their time facing wildfires of emotion and conflict. The responsibility for conflict belongs to the entire leadership of the church, and leaders must claim it as such in order to heal the conflict. Such responsibility relates to the communal nature of the Body of Christ; it is never the problem of one or two individuals. Conflict may also grow because of a failure in skill development in some area (for example, communication, role clarification, administration, and/or boundary formation), and therefore is the product of incompetence, not malevolence.

We tend to take conflict very personally, even if we rarely take sufficient personal responsibility to develop better mediation skills. We say, "What did I do wrong that everyone in the church is angry at me?" Or we say, "John seemed like such a nice person until we made him chair of that committee. Now he is a thorn in my side." Or when we are deeply enmeshed in the conflict, we externalize our personal feelings by saying, "Those people are evil!" Such statements never reflect reality.

In this introduction, I want you to begin to understand three truths that will transform our unfruitful paranoia into positive behavior:

- **Even the smallest group or congregation is a complex social system.** We may recognize that we inadvertently struck the match that started the conflagration of the current conflict and we may even feel guilty, but thousands of past interactions (some of which may have occurred long before we became part of this group) stacked the wood and doused it with gasoline. Congregations embrace many gifts, much strength, and a few weaknesses. Leaders should not assume causal responsibility for everything that happens. Remembering the complexity of the social system is a first step toward transformation. When we remember this social complexity, we find it easier to become a non-defensive listener and to understand all that lies beneath the surface of the current conflict.

- **We need to discuss who we are and how we will behave together.** Healthy groups take time to talk about their identity as a group. They create covenants and agreements concerning their values, their expectations, and the processes by which they will make decisions. These discussions solidify the loving relationships that give cohesiveness to Christ's church. From time to time, people also need to verbalize their level of commitment to their joint task(s). These discussions enable us to limit disruptive behavior and build team spirit. When in conflict, our goal should be to seek a harmonious end to the conflict and to establish a forum for ongoing discussions about our identity and purpose and the ways our identity calls us to behave and interact with one another.

- **Whatever we are doing now is probably wrong.** As a young pastor, my first impulse when faced with conflict was either to try to fix the individuals in conflict or to escape from the scene. Experience taught me that we cannot fix people and that I cannot grow or become a better leader if I withdraw. The value of surviving conflict, and not escaping it, is that we come to trust that the Holy Spirit is present even when tempers flare and meetings become painful. Each conflict that we encounter is one of the things that God has promised to "work for the good of those who love God . . ." (Romans 8:28). We lead others and ourselves to peace by seeking to understand the complex systems underlying the current conflict and by initiating dialogues that establish how the fellowship will behave in the future.

I now see my own incompetence in a variety of conflicts that I have experienced as a church leader, a husband, a father, a child, and a member of various groups and communities. Recognizing my ignorance has led me to read voraciously books about peacemaking, conflict resolution, and the art of cooperation. It has also made me hesitant to offer my own insights. Like the father in the Berenstain Bears children's books, I primarily offer my own actions as a lesson of what not to do.

Current thinking about conflict resolution in the church borrows heavily from family-systems theory. Other insights about the nature of organizational conflict come from the business world. The church is unique, however, when it comes to conflict because we hold as primary our commission to make disciples for Christ (Matthew 28:19). The formation of disciples requires both a focus on loving relationships and a priority for fulfilling our mission. Our mission includes a people and a task. Above all else, our witness is from God. The recognized positives of church life (such as spiritual growth, community outreach, and comfort in times of sorrow) are all the products of processes that merge mission and people through the power of the Holy Spirit.

I believe that God allows conflict to occur in the church because we also enjoy the gift of free will. While longevity of conflict often reflects our incompetence, conflict is never a form of divine retribution. It may help to think of conflict as the pain that forces us to change. In every change, we become aware of things we need to learn and actions we need to take. Inevitably, the opportunities for transformation and growth are greatest when controversy and change are at their height. At this critical point, ordinary people like you and me are called to become wise leaders who model our faith by praising God in the midst of the flames (Daniel 3:25), and we seek ways to address the conflict. We use conflict's heat to refine the congregation's mission vision. We find the courage to purge inappropriate relationships and sometimes even break fellowship with individuals whose misconduct has tainted the whole. Most of all, we seek to discern God's purpose and become more dependent upon God's grace than we were before.

Conflict, as much as I hate it, is not a malevolent thing in itself. Conflict is not the product of sinister or mysterious forces; rather, it is a manageable byproduct of organizational life. Conflict appears in familiar patterns and at predictable points in every congregation's history. Conflict is sometimes a strong medicine and it has power either to kill or to cure the patient for God's glory. Conflict may sidetrack gifted church leaders and make ineffective for a season the witness that a congregation makes. When leaders take an intentional and positive approach to these difficulties, the church emerges healthier and more joyful. That which hindered the mission of the congregation is now a place that witnesses to healing grace.

Sometimes, conflict is nature's way of thinning the herd. I saw a cartoon that depicted a pair of lions and a radar detector. As a herd of antelope stampedes past the lions, one lion says, "Okay, we go for the one on the left. He's down to twenty-seven miles per hour on this pass." The way lions seek out the animal that is tired or weak reminds me of the way certain conflicts pop up in congregations that are running spiritually empty. When a congregation loses its passion for God, it often falls victim to what I call "stupid conflicts." Perhaps two lifelong members of the church suddenly square off over some trivial issue that has nothing to do with the purpose of the church or its ministry. No one appreciates the ruckus stirred up by these two pillars of the church squaring off, but at least something interesting is happening at Old First Church. As another example of a non-issue, I think of a conflict that erupted over the particular hue of the carpet in the sanctuary: Would the color be slate blue or Williamsburg blue? Both shades were beautiful. Neither color was more or less beautiful than the other, but that color choice initiated conflict, which called us back to consider the purpose of the church within that community. Conflict sometimes provides energy to a congregation that has become apathetic. For any organization, the loss of momentum is painful. The explosion of a church fight gets things moving again, though often in the wrong direction. Chapter one will deal with ways to manage this pattern.

Other churches develop a culture of high commitment and a zeal for the Lord. Just when they seem to be making great progress towards their goals, they run smack into the brick wall of conflict. In type "A" congregations, conflict usually results from a substantial difference of opinion over a key issue. Two groups may have radically different ideas about what it means to be a church. One group wants to break ground on a new addition, while opposing voices wish to send the architects back to their drawing boards to develop cheaper alternatives. These conflicts burn hotter and hotter as each side seeks to get the church to make the "right" decision about the issue. The solution, however, does not lie in choosing the right path. It lies in the church's accepting that the process it follows in making decisions is more important than any given decision.

The positive goal of the conflict is to force church leaders to step away from their positions and discover again how to honor each other as people first. Chapter two focuses on how to keep on task while developing a more loving fellowship. (Another book in this series, *Jesus' New Command*, also describes this task.)

Still other churches find themselves so relationally focused that they view every task in terms of the personalities of the individuals doing that activity. The issue, for example, is not maintaining the church landscape at the best price, but whose feelings it would hurt if we hire Mr. Jones instead of Mr. Roberts. In small-membership churches, this type of controversy often pits the acknowledged patriarch or matriarch of the church against a group of newcomers. Mid-sized churches fight the relationship wars between opposing groups, often with the pastor triangulated between the groups. Larger churches get hung up on the personalities of the various staff persons and how the current senior pastor fails to walk in the honored footsteps of his or her predecessor. These battles between cliques derail the decision-making process of the congregation. In the midst of a personality-related conflict, our first instinct is to try to get people to like each other and play nice. When this approach fails, as it always does, we learn again that no one can *fix* someone else's behavior. We cannot stop two people from fighting. However, we can manage the effects of their problem has on the total congregational system. The positive value of these relational conflicts is that they force us to develop behavior covenants and organizational processes that work for everyone instead of tailoring them to the current personalities. Chapter three examines how to get out of the personality rut.

The Soils

Jesus tells a parable about seed falling on differing types of soil (Matthew 13:1-9). Problems directly related to the character of the soil limited the young plant's growth and potential for fruitfulness. Thin soil promoted quick growth but failed to sustain it. Rich soil created other problems for the seed by permitting weeds to take over. This same imagery works well in describing how congregational culture (the soil) relates to the Holy Spirit's intention (the seed) to form disciples for Christ through the church. Thin soil is analogous to a congregational culture that is highly task-oriented, but lacks sufficient emphasis upon the interpersonal relationships that will sustain people as they grow in faith. The conflicts that emerge in this type of church usually relate to substantial differences of opinion. In contrast, the congregational culture that focuses on its rich fellowship, ignoring its missional task, is vulnerable to family squabbles and the formation of cliques. The conflicts that arise in a church directly relate to the culture a congregation maintains.

As individuals, our temperaments tend to lean toward either a task orientation or a relational orientation. Consider two persons who come home from the same church meeting. One says, "What a waste of time. We didn't accomplish anything." The other says, "This was a good meeting. Everyone had a chance to say something, and we got to know each other better." Organizations, committees, and fellowships are a blend of differing temperaments, but often one orientation becomes predominant. For a church, task versus people (relationship) orientation is one component of congregational culture. One outcome of major conflict is that it shifts congregational culture, sometimes for the better, but not always. Conflict may also lead to the departure from power, and sometimes from the church as well, of people who represent a particular temperament. In their absence, other previously unheard voices emerge to shape or reform the orientation of the church system. If we are people-oriented, we may feel bad about what has happened even if the cultural shift has improved the effectiveness of the church.

It is helpful to chart task orientation versus relational orientation for a given congregation (see chart at the end of this introduction). We note that when task orientation is high and people dismiss the relational values, we often praise church leaders for their capacity to "get 'er done." Those in power, even if they are not personally task-oriented, listen to the voices of others to remain on task. Invariably, they skip some important step in the church's democratic process, and controversy erupts. This thin task-oriented soil may also foster the rapid development of opposing camps with substantial differences of opinion about what the church should be doing. Here again, lapses in communication and the suspicion that others may be violating the rules of the game add fuel to the fire. The "irreconcilable differences" form of controversy emerges (see quadrant one).

In the opposite corner of the chart is a congregational culture that values relationships so highly that the task of making disciples and being in mission to transform the world is rarely stated (quadrant three). These churches are like families that smother their teenagers with unreasonable expectations. Pastors in these congregations, particularly newly arrived ones, often complain about the "pillars of the church" controlling or manipulating them. On a positive note, these churches can be rich and fertile places engaged in the long-term task of nurturing the faith of their weakest member. But they also nurture cliques and encourage the keeping of secrets. Conflict may simmer under the surface for years. When conflict emerges, it will inevitably involve a person with formal authority, such as the pastor or a newly elected chairperson of a committee, who attempts to accomplish something without the approval of a key person who has relational status (informal authority) in the church.

There are three other places on the chart. The bottom left square marks the territory of congregations that are neither driven to accomplish tasks nor tightly bound by loving relationships (quadrant two). This is the rocky soil of spiritual apathy that neither gives root to missional tasks nor nurturing relationships. Low attendance and poor stewardship characterize life in this square. The church may be living off an endowment or settling into a routine of only doing maintenance of its facilities. It greets each new initiative with the words, "Do we have to do this?" Some cultures of apathy are the products of over-functioning clergy who do everything that should be done in the church. Other congregations drop into apathy as a safe mode for healing after some trauma. They may be recovering from pastoral misconduct or be in a state of exhaustion after a church fight. A third type of church that often falls into this category is the "historic" church. The building where the congregation meets may have some architectural or historical significance, real or imagined. This need to preserve the past becomes a damp rag that smothers the normal flame of passion for mission, witness, and Christian fellowship.

These churches are only peaceful for a season. The over-functioning pastor will one day leave or burn out. The traumatized church will one day face whatever secrets or critical issues it failed to resolve during its crisis. The historic church will eventually face the fact that people do not go to museums to worship the living God or to discover the warmth of Christian fellowship by looking at the walls. Churches in a state of spiritual apathy provide fertile soil for conflict, even though they are by nature risk-averse. What Isaac Newton failed to discover is that a body at rest attracts forces that will keep it from remaining at rest. The most powerful social force that leads groups into controversy is the pain of boredom. Pseudo-harmony is mind numbing. It eventually leads someone to do or say something outrageous just to stir up something. Churches in the lower-left quadrant are most subject to what I referred to earlier as "stupid" conflicts.

When congregations resolve a conflict, whether it is minor or substantial, most return to their home-place. This is the middle square in the chart. It is the place where they hold in check the pressure to be either overly task-oriented or people-oriented. They only attempt those tasks that do not jeopardize the unity of the fellowship. Those who value the intimacy of their own small circle of friends are accepting new members into their groups so they can accomplish some tasks together. A congregation will often enter this state of equilibrium when it receives a new pastor. The "honeymoon" period is one where both extremes are waiting to see which direction the new pastor will lead. A congregation emerging from an "irreconcilable differences" (task-oriented) form of controversy will seek a safe home-place where they can keep divergent ideas in check. Similarly, a church that has had a family-feud type of conflict (relationship-oriented) will look for a home-place that has enough missional drive to keep everyone engaged in the common task. The problem with home-places and honeymoons is they cannot and should not last for long. In the home-place, the task-oriented members are working with one hand tied behind their backs, and the people-oriented folk are anxiously waiting to root themselves in their own comfort zone. Home is the outwardly happy place where no one is entirely happy.

On rare occasions, a church will enter a fourth quadrant where they value both mission and fellowship. The military saying, "Mission first, people always," characterizes this growing place. Unlike the second quadrant of apathy, it is passionately spiritual. Like the task-oriented first quadrant, it strives for missional action, but does so without sacrificing loving relationships. Good leaders realize that their goal is not to guide the church towards a balanced happy home base, but to merge mission and fellowship into a holy, open-ended alliance. This involves capturing the creativity and diversity of people and freeing them to make full use of their gifts, including their temperaments. It also involves forsaking the shallower forms of community life. Shallow fellowships are based on people relating in homogeneous groupings or having limits to their vulnerability or the transparency of their motives. People in shallow communities do not commit themselves to work together on goals that are more compelling than those they hold in their personal lives. In contrast, tight-knit but diverse teams that accomplish challenging and awesome tasks (and in the process, build a sustainable community of faith) characterize life in this fourth quadrant.

Good News

Conflict can lead to growth. This sentence runs counter to what most people believe. In fact, the only way into the fourth quadrant is to resolve conflict purposefully while avoiding pseudo-harmony. Beyond healing is growth. Churches often avoid the real potential. Laity, pastors, and judicatory leaders (such as district superintendents) consistently seek to resolve conflict by moving the congregation back towards its home-place. They broker solutions that pacify the adversaries of the conflict but fail to develop a unifying merger of missional goals and tight-knit fellowship groups. The history of most churches is a meandering tale of how they climbed for a few years onto the safe high ground of pseudo-harmony, then fell into periods of task orientation, apathy, or cliquish fellowship ending in conflict, and finally returned to the home-place.

Churches tolerate this unproductive, repetitive pattern because unmanaged conflict is painful. How much pain you feel as a church leader because of parish conflicts will depend upon two factors:

- **Your personal temperament:** If adrenaline causes you to "flee" rather than "fight" in tense situations, you may be conflict-averse. If "duck and cover" is your favorite position in an argument, you may be prone to moving towards quick resolutions rather than pushing for productive change.

- **Your personal investment in the situation:** The church council may frame the issue being brought to them in purely objective terms and prefaced with the remark, "Don't take this personally . . . ." It may involve lowering the budgeted allowance for choir music or the upgrading of carpet in the parsonage. If you, however, are the choir director or the parson, you are likely to take it personally. Mediation and management of conflict usually require the involvement of people who do not have a stake in the issue or a fear of the personalities involved.

Getting out of this unproductive cycle of resolving issues only to return to an unstable home-place will require church leaders to commit to team-building strategies that will challenge their conflict-averse temperaments. Churches will need to modify their behaviors intentionally. The congregation will need to weave transparency and direct communication into its culture. It helps to recognize that times of conflict are times of transition. When the church is in transition, the leadership needs to know that the decision-making process will be far more important than any particular decision. While our first impulse will be to solve the problem that prompted the controversy, a healthier plan is to work to improve the way the congregation thinks about its business and its fellowship and to let the particular issues resolve themselves.

The pain of conflict relates to what Peter Steinke describes in

Congregational Leadership in Anxious Times: Being Calm and Courageous No Matter What (The Alban Institute, 2006) as "congregational anxiety." Beyond our personal feelings about a situation, there is a larger group with emotional tension. Congregations are organic entities. In times of uncertainty, their collective anxiety grows. When there is evidence that they have made a poor decision or that the congregation has treated someone shamefully, anxiety unifies these normally independent, rational individuals into an odd fellowship that may behave foolishly. Problems with easy solutions become great weights or albatrosses hung around the necks of the church council. These members become quick to express anger and slow to demonstrate trust. They reject wise counsel from outsiders and tolerate uncivil behavior from their own. The church's actions speak more about their collective mindset than about how any individual feels. Paradoxically, in times of high anxiety, one observes both a rush towards legalism and a laxness to discipline outrageous behavior. Often irrationality runs rampant, and the first task is to create an extensive set of rules that have nothing to do with civility.

Getting to the productive fourth quadrant of the diagram at the end of this introduction always involves understanding and managing congregational anxiety. For this reason, the first chapter of this book will not deal with the particular conflicts that arise from having an overly task or people-oriented congregational culture. Instead, it will address the brutish nature of the church when anxiety has driven it beyond rational behavior.

Isn't It Always the Pastor's Fault? (A Tongue-in-Cheek Question)

My system for categorizing congregations into one of four quadrants needs to consider another question: How does the pastor's own personality influence the congregation? Like all complicated systems, the local church contains inertia. When a pastor arrives at a new parish, he or she will find the congregation has its own customs, procedures for making decisions, and mutually-held values. A mill-town congregation with a blue-collar tradition may be so comfortable with task-oriented, top-down procedures that they let the pastor tell them what programs they will do and when. Ten miles away in a rural setting there may exist a relation/consensus-oriented, small congregation that holds an hour-long meeting in the parking lot after worship to choose the right date for the strawberry festival.

The extremely task-oriented pastor may shift the congregational culture towards a new way of doing things. He or she may be entirely unaware of this pastoral influence. The choices suggested to the lay leadership committee, the order of items on the church council's agenda, and the time the pastor gives to each announcement or meeting notification will subtly shift the culture. Meanwhile, the relationship-oriented pastor arriving in a task-oriented church may influence their process by the way he or she expresses a concern for the feelings of those not elected to office. The pastor teaches the agenda-oriented chairpersons of each committee how to appreciate and value the relational messages that percolate through a congregation because of the pastor's example.

After three to six years, most congregations begin to resemble the temperament of their pastor. Some environmental factors may lengthen this time. In my region, there are places where the major employer has had an influence on the culture of every organization in the town. A congregation that has experienced a series of short-term pastorates or has experienced clergy misconduct may be reluctant to shift the culture that has enabled it to survive. Part of the reason for this book is to help pastors understand and appreciate the existing culture of a congregation. Conflict often arises when the clergyperson believes that the congregation's way of doing things is wrong and must change immediately. On the other hand, when the church and its pastor share the same temperament and similar cultural values, they can become dangerously comfortable in their quadrant. It is not good for a church to become so relationship-oriented that it forsakes its Christian mission or to become so focused on its task that it fails to build a healthy fellowship. Sometimes burned-out or lackluster pastors move to churches in quadrant two, the place of apathy. No one should express surprise when stupid conflicts end the life of a congregation in this situation.

The Layer Cake of Conflict

If we can think of various quadrants of congregational conflict as the layers of a cake, the icing is the anxiety the congregation feels towards change. Congregational culture is a relatively stable entity, baked and formed in historical layers. When one digs through the archives of a church, one can find in the narrative layers a time when the congregation was grounded firmly in a task-oriented (quadrant one) mindset. They built additions to the edifice, sent out missionaries, and accomplished goal after goal. Then come layers where fellowship groups take precedence, or periods when nothing much happened and apathy ruled by default. Between each layer is a sweet (if you are an outside church consultant), and sometimes chaotic, icing of high anxiety.

Any discussion of congregational conflict must consider the dynamics of change and anxiety. Very few people, and even fewer congregations, innately resist change. However, no one, no matter how adventurous, is immune to anxiety. For a variety of reasons, change often leads to anxiety. For individuals, this process may feel convoluted; for congregational systems, the process seems downright mysterious. Many church-conflict books attempt to explain how the icing of anxiety is mixed. The important concept, however, is that congregational anxiety comes from within the system. To begin to manage and heal conflict, we need to attribute anxiety to the way the entire congregation is responding to change, rather than judging it as a character flaw in the individual expressing it at the moment.

Having Our Cake and Eating It Too

Confession is good for the soul: Let us now say together that there have been times when we rejoiced to see conflict continue because it fostered our agenda or met a personal need. Conflicts would not last long in the church if there weren't some sweet morsels served up with every argument. I know a pastor whose average tenure at each church was three years. That was all the time it took for him to split each congregation into a group that loved him and a group that hated him. With every word of praise that the first group spoke, he had the satisfaction of knowing that he was almost divine; with every criticism the other group spoke, he tasted the joy of martyrdom.

While most people do not exercise that degree of obvious game-playing, family-systems theory alerts us to the benefits that we enjoy from maintaining conflict. If nothing else, having our community divide into those we agree with and those we are at odds with adds a sense of structure and order to our worldview. We feel more secure knowing that "so and so" is always wrong because they are a liberal, a fundamentalist, an outsider, an insider, or because they are related to this or that family. We think if we can pigeonhole them or apply a label to their views, then we no longer need to treat them as people of equal worth. The painful aspects of conflict can force us to recognize the diversity of experience and viewpoints that every congregation represents. Too often, the sweetness of putting others down robs dessert of its virtue.

I do not hear in Jesus' words a disdain for conflict as much as I hear a rebuke for the joy we take in having our cake of controversy and eating it too. He constantly challenged his disciples to see others as people of holy value, no matter what their circumstances or their opinions. Imagine someone traveling with Jesus who enjoys the security of the hatred that exists between Jew and Samaritan, between those who keep Torah as Pharisees and the unclean tax collectors, between Palestinian natives and Roman soldiers. Hardly a day goes by when Jesus doesn't do something to get you out of your familiar box of prejudice. By word and deed, Jesus teaches you to love everyone. This is the real task of a peacemaker. Peacemakers do not end conflict by getting everyone to agree; they bring mercy and healing into every relationship, demonstrating a life lived in recognition of the value of each individual.

Over the years, I have read a number of authors who present methods for dealing with troublemakers, but not always in the way of peace. I also have found resources to help manipulate group process to get the results that you want. Such approaches now sadden me because they show little respect for other human beings created in God's image. I am convinced that church leaders, both clergy and lay, need to study peacemaking and the nature of conflict, not because something is wrong with their congregations, but because these concepts are central to the gospel of our Lord. Unfortunately, we tend to think that when people fight there is a problem to fix, rather than a lesson to learn. Our current approach to conflict demonstrates a basic incompetence as we seek to heal divisions in the Body of Christ. David never viewed Saul as a maniac who needed containment. Perhaps that is what made him such an effective musician and therapist for Saul. David simply loved Saul and played the best he could for the manic king. If nothing else, my hope is that what follows will help you as a church leader to keep playing your song through times of dissension and times of peace. May you discover, even in conflict, the merciful presence of God.

Congregational Culture and Conflict

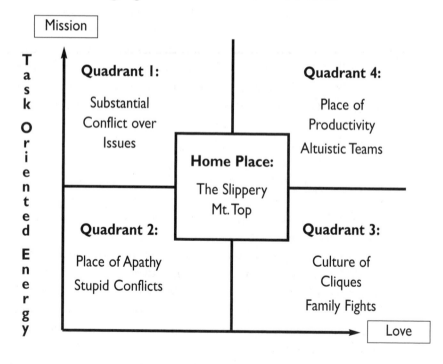

CHAPTER ONE

Anxiety and Change: The Icing on the Cake

May I walk in beauty—beauty behind me, beauty in front of me,
beauty above and beneath me, and beauty all around me.

Traditional Navajo Prayer

Jesse took a donkey loaded with bread, a skin of wine and a young
goat and sent them by his son David to Saul . . . . whenever the evil
spirit from God came upon Saul, David took the lyre and played it
with his hand, and Saul would be relieved and feel better, and the
evil spirit would depart from him.

I Samuel 16:20, 23

The story of David playing his harp before Saul has an interesting parallel in Matthew's Gospel. Herod the Great, like Saul, used his political and military savvy to unify the nation of Israel. His throne was secure from outsiders; no one could defeat Herod except Herod. The trouble with both Saul and Herod is that they had streaks of madness.

Charming and gracious hosts one moment and paranoid schizophrenics the next' they murdered their children, mistrusted their friends, and abused their court musicians. Augustus Caesar reportedly said that it was better to be Herod's pig than to be Herod's son. (See, for example, *Good News of Great Joy* by William Barclay.) Herod's command to slaughter the infants of Bethlehem makes as much military sense as Saul's fitful pursuit of David in the wilderness (1 Samuel 19–30). It is easy, however, in our yearly reading of the Christmas story to put all the blame on Herod as an individual. We miss the powerful role Herod played in the social context. Thirty years after the death of Herod the Great, the stage was set for Jesus to participate in a similar conflict with a grandson of Herod the Great, Herod Agrippa. After Saul's death, David discovered he was not immune to a different form of murderous insanity: David's lust for Bathsheba cost Uriah his life. To understand conflict, both on the biblical stage and in the church, we need to look beyond these large personalities and discover what is going on in the congregational system and in its social context.

Matthew wrote that the appearance of the wise men troubled not only Herod but also all of Jerusalem (Matthew 2:3). The people wanted their king to be happy. Herod the Great had ruled for over thirty years before the wise men arrived seeking the newborn king. The shopkeepers in the marketplace usually want to preserve the status quo. In a similar way, when Saul's advisors brought young David into the palace, they did not expect him to change the system. They only wanted to mitigate the effects of Saul's illness.

In every congregation, many factors work to maintain the current organization system, including tradition, inertia, church polity, democratic process, spiritual discernment, and reason. The church never can be purely spiritual or reasonable in its decision-making. There is always a great flywheel of past precedents and historical baggage. A family system of interpersonal relationships keeps this flywheel in motion. The gyroscopic inertia of this system allows—in fact, even requires—eccentric characters to remain in office for a long time.

To clarify this image, think of a crowded schoolhouse merry-go-round, with a dominant child sitting on its axis. A bully can use the centrifugal force of the spinning merry-go-round to oust any contender. The other children on the ride may not support the bully, but they enjoy keeping the wheel spinning. They have a cooperative system that doesn't need the bully, but inadvertently keeps the bully in power. Over time, the bully's antics may trouble some of the children. They don't accept the bully's boast that his authority is what keeps the whole wheel turning. A few of the children may even call out to an outsider to come onboard and unseat the bully. The group as a whole, however, is not willing to stop the system that perpetuates the abuser's power.

As David carries his harp into Saul's palace, he quickly learns two things: Saul is still king and the system doesn't really want to change. Church leaders often find themselves in similar situations. When a new pastor arrives in a conflicted congregation, the newcomer often encounters a well-entrenched Herod or Saul. The members of the congregation or a judicatory leader may have told the new pastor that his or her first job will be to "bell the cat" or deal with the perceived troublemaker. We need to resist the temptation to fixate on the absurd behavior of the bully. The real job of the church leader, like it or not, is to help the system become healthier. One of the important themes of this series of books (Congregational Leadership Empowered for Change) is that all true leadership is systemic. In some sense, the entire congregation empowers the person who behaves badly. This does not excuse people's behavior, nor does it make them less responsible for their actions. Instead, it alerts the wise leader to the need to dig deeper and root out the systemic causes of conflict.

Leaders who attempt to bring about change in a congregation that has recently lost its resident Saul or Herod face a similar dynamic. Long-term pastors often become ringleaders in the congregational system. Their influence lingers on long after they leave the congregation. There may be hesitancy on the church council's part to discuss serious issues without wondering, "What would our old pastor do?" The former pastor may even receive their phone calls, but the congregational system, not the former pastor, is the real culprit. Another person may quickly fill the

vacuum created by the exit of one dominant personality. In every congregational system, congregations always overestimate power of the
dominant personalities while they are in office, but will consistently
underestimate the ongoing legacy of any abuses leaders commit. This is
why interim ministers and transitional consultants rarely are called. In
my own denomination, the United Methodist Church, we would rather
follow clergy misconduct with an unwitting new pastor who becomes an
unintentional interim (or scapegoat), rather than plan for a period of
transition. Here again, we tend to focus on the individual who misbehaves rather than seek to understand how the clergy/congregation
relationship plays out in that system. One question we need to ask: What
was latent in the congregational system that allowed them to be vulnerable for abuse?

A third situation occurs when a bully invites a more moderate person to share their power while knowing that the bully can stay in charge
by controlling the surrogate. One historical example of this is visible in
the appointment by King Henry II of his friend and chancellor, Thomas
Becket, to be archbishop of Canterbury. Since Thomas had loyally served
the king for many years, Henry assumed that Thomas would exercise his
new office as a loyal puppet of the throne. Thomas, however, immediately transferred his full loyalty to the church and fearlessly challenged
the king's authority over ecclesiastical matters. The resulting conflict
made for memorable drama (see, for example, *Becket*, an Oscar-winning
film directed by Peter Glenville, which starred Richard Burton and Peter
O'Toole) and left Becket a martyr. Again, these historic personalities,
however legendary, are not the real story. Contemporary issues often
reenact the same conflict between church and state. Do political office
holders have any ongoing obligation to the religious groups that funded
their campaigns? Should the church deny Holy Communion to candi-
dates whose political stands differ from official church positions? How
much latitude do clergy have in voicing their political opinions from the
pulpit? Inside a congregation, there is a similar tension between key
church leaders and individuals (often the pastor) who voice divergent
opinions. The dominant personalities are quick to point out that they
"own" the offending individual because they pay his salary or in some

way secured her position. Others remain loyal to the system's bullies, even when those people do not actually hold a church office or represent the majority opinion on the issue.

Upon arriving in a new parish, many pastors find themselves courted by a dominant personality who wants them to act as their surrogate. The week after Pastor Sally announced her new appointment to Hopeful Glen United Methodist Church, she received a call from John Luke, the chairperson of the finance committee [note these names are fictional, but, the events portrayed are common enough]. Mr. Luke, in a warm and friendly voice, offered to drive the two hours to her town and take her out for lunch. Even though she wouldn't begin her work at Hopeful Glen for another three months, he said that it would be helpful for them to meet together and "get on the same page" concerning the church's finances. The ensuing lunch eased any concerns Pastor Sally had about Mr. Luke, as he provided her with a wealth of useful information. He mentioned the good relationship he had enjoyed with the out-going pastor and pledged to do whatever he could to make the transition smooth. Over the next six months, Sally found herself depending upon the wise council of the fatherly Mr. Luke, and he in turn did much to gain acceptance for her from those church members who had been reluctant to receive a woman pastor. It wasn't until the yearly budgeting process that Pastor Sally realized what John Luke meant when he said, "We do things our own way here at Hopeful Glen." He drafted the budget without any input from other committees and presented it as a *fait accompli*. Later, she learned that some members of the church council had significant concerns, but that they were waiting for her to question the document first. Over the next two years, she watched in horror as John persistently used the adopted budget to prevent any expenditure that he personally did not approve. As her third fall approached, she steeled herself for a major conflict. Pastor Sally stated frankly, "Either we have a fair budgeting process this year, or I will personally see that John Luke is not nominated for Finance chair." Meanwhile, her district superintendent received a call from the Staff-Parish Relations Committee, who requested a move for Pastor Sally because she never quite settled into "the way we do things around here" at Hopeful Glen.

David as a Transitional Leader

David is anointed king of Israel in I Samuel 16, but he doesn't assume the throne until twenty chapters and half a decade later. David's long transitional period mirrors the time in the United Methodist tradition between the appointment of a new pastor and the physical exit of the former pastor. This period of overlap can last for years if the exiting clergy retires or relocates nearby. Long or chaotic transitions also occur when the exiting pastor dies in office, when some act of misconduct has disgraced him or her, or when the exiting pastor has "rigged" things in some way so that his or her successor will fail. Just as David did not receive the throne when Samuel splashed oil on his head, so also the actual exchange of leadership authority does not transfer from one clergy person to the next when the bishop reads their name at annual conference. The dissonance between the authority that pastors have on paper (known as positional power) and that which their new churches enables them to act out of in their office (their permitted sphere of influence) underlies many church conflicts. Even when there hasn't been a recent change in leadership, conflict often is rooted in the unwillingness of people to transfer allegiance and responsibilities to those whom the church designates, via its organizational chart, to do a particular task. This annoying aspect of the human condition is rarely a matter of people failing to like or trust the new person. It is an unwillingness to release the emotions, good or ill, that they feel towards the person(s) who once held that office and to accept the fact that the new person will wear their role differently. Memorable personalities cast long shadows, which do not diminish with reports of incompetence or with affirmations of the capabilities of successors. Unfortunately, many of us attempt to speed the transition into the power of office by alternately putting down our predecessor and putting forward our own credentials. These actions prepare the stage for future conflict. They work counter to the natural process of letting people shift their allegiance as they observe how the new person redefines the role associated with the position or office.

Think about the loss of momentum and chaos that often occur in transitions such as pastoral change. It reminds me of Marc Antony's eulogy for Caesar: "The evil that men do lives after them; the good is oft interred with their bones" (Shakespeare: *Julius Caesar*, Act III scene 2). Shakespeare sets this speech as a cathartic moment in the play. The people of Rome will not move forward to accept the new leadership until they deal with their anxiety about how the old leadership was removed. Congregations that request that a pastor be reassigned elsewhere will often find themselves embroiled in conflict or debilitated by an inability to make critical decisions in the following years. The pastoral-relations committee may have been wise in seeking a change, but the congregational system is still in need of healing and atonement.

Church leaders should take certain transitional steps to address the conflict inherent when there are unusual circumstances surrounding a pastoral change. In Shakespeare's play, the role of Marc Antony is similar to that of an interim minister or transitional consultant. Rome is on the verge of civil war. Marc Antony cannot defuse the anxiety of the crowd, nor can he bring about a reasonable compromise between those who supported Caesar and those who murdered him. He can and does, however, lead the crowd to act more appropriately than they would otherwise. He also chooses carefully the historical allusions of his speech to set the stage for the crowd's transfer of allegiance to Octavius. We find in Antony's speech the following transitional steps:

- He states his own role as a mediator (or interim), not supporting either side in the controversy but seeking to establish a just process for the future of Rome.

- He leads the people through a reflection on their history.

- He depolarizes "us versus them," black and white thinking, showing an alternative, centrist view which embraces both sides.

- He accentuates the shared identity of the crowd as citizens of Rome.

- He equips them to act justly (punishing the murderers of Caesar) while preparing for needed leadership change.

When a dominant person in a lay leadership role decides to step down or moves out of office, the congregation faces similar dynamics to those experienced during pastoral change. Sometimes, an exiting leader may continue to work behind the scenes to sabotage the new office holder or to stymie the process of nominating a replacement. Sometimes, he or she may champion a puppet as a replacement. I think it is extremely important that congregations develop a culture that expects leadership rotation. Lavishly recognize long-term office holders when they step down. Publicly inform new leaders of any term limit related to their position. Further, hold a yearly dedication service of all church volunteers and include a covenant to mentor others into leadership.

David's attitude and actions towards Saul are striking and instructive. He constantly refers to Saul as "the Lord's Anointed" and is careful to display publicly his deference to Saul's throne. Few pastors seem to realize that when they speak ill of their predecessor, they are diminishing the respect that people have for the pastoral office. David cannot claim any authority for his own actions as an anointed leader without recognizing the authority that same position gave to Saul. David goes a step further by being extremely guarded towards those who want to praise him at the expense of Saul. Instead, he leads the nation in honoring Saul's life. David wisely recognizes that the people need the opportunity to express the depths of their emotional attachment to their first king. As we will see later, we cannot change history, but we can heal and manage it. We cannot erase and dare not ignore the experiences that people had under a previous leader, but we can manage and celebrate them in a way that confesses the bad and honors the good. The reluctance a congregation expresses towards new ideas and the resistance they offer towards change directly relates to the unresolved baggage that they carry. Helping individuals and groups speak about the past is a tremendous tool in empowering them towards progressive action.

Hidden Anxiety

Just as we each experience tension, stress, and anxiety in our personal lives, congregations experience systemic anxiety. There is a tension in the body as a whole, which is separate from the way any particular individual feels. This congregational anxiety is like static electricity. As I walk across the carpet, I may accumulate several thousand volts of electrical charge and distribute it across my body. Yet each of my organs keeps functioning as before: my stomach still processes its Danish and coffee; my hand still holds the newspaper; my mind still processes the comics. Then I reach the doorknob and the air turns blue with a terrific spark. Should I blame my hand, the doorknob, or my shoes?

Occasionally, we will observe someone we know well who is acting now in a way that is not in keeping with his or her character. We may inquire and discover that something has happened at home that sparked the behavioral change. For a moment, we realize that this person is not simply the colleague who sits beside us at the board meeting, but is a member of another system. She arrives every morning pushing back into her subconscious mind the anxiety she feels about her rebellious teenager and her father who is in the early stages of Alzheimer's. As she enters the boardroom, I am biting into the last Danish, the one she has been anticipating as hers. Suddenly the air turns blue and fills with a terrific spark.

None of us, even after years of psychoanalysis, is fully able to disengage our childhood memories or to ignore the way our current family system influences our response to situations outside the home. Each individual who agrees to sit on our church council brings with him or her a dozen or more other relationships, which, while invisible, are significant. Each time the council needs to make a decision, we hope to utilize a solid threefold process of prayerful discernment, careful fact-gathering, and reasoned discussion. We bring to the table our personal spirituality, the wisdom gained from prior experiences, and a willingness to speak our thoughts. We rarely fulfill this intention. Many things can push some or all of the group out of its intended decision making mind and into a state where anxiety is the key player.

Consider the following factors in contrast to how we hope to make decisions or participate in an organization:

- **Proximity:** How close an issue is to where we live affects the anxiety we bring to the group process. Mary will have a hard time keeping the dynamics of her family system out of her mind during the Council's discussion concerning the leadership of the youth group her son attends. Pastor Jones will find it dif-

ficult to be a non-anxious spiritual leader at the trustee meeting
while they discuss changes to the parsonage. Jake may have a
hard time participating in worship after the church disposed of
the hymnals given in memory of his beloved grandparents.

- **Time Stress:** The urgency attached to any given situation alters
  the way committee members process it. A committee will place
  greater importance on insignificant items when they appear
  urgent. Some church leaders have mastered the art of presenting things at the last minute so the church council voices its
  gratitude for how busy the leader has been rather than exercis-
  ing its discernment about how fruitful the project will be.

- **Past Failures:** Every committee meeting will have its quorum
  of ghosts present. People remember similar things that have
  failed in that congregation, similar risks that have adversely
  affected the fortunes of each committee member, and the
  stories they may have heard of costly mistakes done elsewhere. The fact that the current item under discussion
  involves different people, resources, and organizational safe-
  guards does not prevent subconscious minds from noting
  narrative similarities and reacting with fear.

- **Authority Issues:** Before any group can function well, there
  needs to be consensus about the level of authority each member has in that group. They should decide the weight that the
  group's decisions will have in the overall scheme of things.
  Some groups intentionally state that they will listen to all
  members and work to maintain equality. Other groups invest
  a higher level of authority in their chairperson, pastor, or eld-
  est members. At any given moment, the anxiety that a
  member feels about his or her relative position in the group
  may overrule that person's ability to make a reasoned contribution to the process. When a number of people in the
  group become unclear about their positions or when a contest between two members vying for authority sidetracks the

group, the general anxiety level rises significantly. The group may also become anxious when it senses another committee may overrule it or say its decisions are subject to approval by the people who really run the church.

• **Foggy Expectations:** Having significant consensus around a concise mission statement and a clear vision about what needs to be done may not solve everything in a congregation, but it sure lowers the general level of anxiety. Every organization needs strategic objectives. We can maintain a false sense of calm by keeping everyone busy, but eventually people want to know that their contributions are making a difference. In speaking about its mission, a congregation sets a general level of expectation for everyone. This allows the congregation to clarify the expectations of each committee and person in leadership. Groups and individuals would prefer to feel that others have high expectations of them rather than face the anxiety present when expectations are absent or abstract.

Each of us needs to be aware of the personal level of anxiety we bring into the group settings where we participate. Try scoring yourself in the table below as you look at each item on the upcoming agenda of a meeting you will be attending.

Closeness to   (near & dear /
Home: (ok) 0 . . . I . . . 2 . . . 3 . . . 4 . . . 5   high anxiety)
Time   (hurried /
Crunch: (ok) 0. . . I . . . 2 . . . 3 . . . 4 . . . 5   high anxiety)
                                            (overwhelmed by the past/
Ghosts: (ok)   0. . . I . . . 2 . . . 3 . . . 4 . . . 5   high anxiety)
Authority   (confusion or competition /
Issues: (ok)   0 . . . I . . . 2 . . . 3 . . . 4 . . . 5   high anxiety)
Clarity about   (unclear/
expectations: (ok) 0 . . . I . . . 2 . . . 3 . . . 4 . . . 5   high anxiety)
                                                   Total score _____

The successful leader seeks first to understand his or her personal experience of anxiety. Having done an honest appraisal of how emotions distort involvement in rational discussion, the leader seeks to create a buffer, differentiating personal sense of anxiety from that of the group. The leader may inform the group of his or her anxiety at appropriate times, using "I" statements. Instead of sharing what others are saying and using the nebulous "they," the leader models an example of willingness to claim and name his or her own experience. Good leaders model transparency and affirm that others may see things differently.

Now, step back and try to score the group's general level of anxiety about the same issues. Keep both numbers and the total score on the agenda as you attend the meeting. Try to notice the body language of the people around you. How well did you predict the points at which tension was evident in the room? How did your anxiety and the level of anxiety in the room relate to the amount of time the group gave to each item? Did the chair limit discussion during moments of tension? Was the group prone to procrastinate or table those items that raised their level of anxiety? Can you find a unifying theme to the issues and words that caused a stir? Did you see faces stiffen or words become terser when the group dealt with money, time, or the prestige of certain participants? Did anyone refer to the feelings of persons not present?

People in groups often multiply, rather than add to, the anxiety level that each individual brings to the table. Some of the members of the group may be highly relationship-oriented or significantly codependent. When they sense anxiety in another person, they may sympathetically mirror or amplify those feelings. The task-oriented person, on the other hand, may be anxious to see the group's authority structure solidify in a way that favors his or her agenda. They also may dismiss concerns about past failures or discussions about who has a personal stake in the issue. This cutting off of discussion and enforcing time restrictions on the group process inadvertently elevates and legitimizes those hidden anxieties.

The Non-Anxious Leader

Just as a lightning rod can prevent disaster by safely channeling electricity to the ground, so the church leader who acts as a non-anxious presence enables decision-making bodies to remain productive in difficult times. This phrase means more than just carrying a peaceful demeanor, though being able to remain unperturbed in the midst of conflict's storm never hurts. The people who model a non-anxious presence also strive to understand and name the sources of the group's anxiety without adding their own fears into the mix. Such leaders are more concerned that the group members develop a healthy process for making decisions than that they decide a particular way on a given issue. They can listen to what people say without becoming defensive. They are present with the group but are at the same time emotionally self-differentiated.

Under normal circumstances, great leaders share their vision and wisdom to help people take action. But when there is conflict or high anxiety, great leaders help the group neutralize the effects of their fears and regain their sanity. The "healing" leader has a different task than the "visionary" leader. Healers deal with process, whereas visionary leaders deal with results. As committees go about their business, they tend to judge themselves by what they accomplish (unless they are fully into quadrant three: culture of relationships). When the collective anxiety level reaches a certain point, however, meetings become painful, decisions flawed, and implementation impossible. The leader may state the committee's goals with clarity and contribute divine inspiration along the way, but the group still has its baggage that will continue to get in the way until a healer enters their process.

The non-anxious, healing leader reminds the group that its chief task is not to perform miracles but to engage in prayerful discernment, careful fact-gathering, and reasoned discussion. Healthy groups do this with the awareness that some of their decisions will be wrong, poorly implemented, or out of sync with the current reality. They note their failures with a sense of humor. They build trust and partnership with each other and their pastoral staff. They are mindful of the boundaries between their bailiwick and that of other committees or groups in the church. They keep reasonable hours and do not engage in frantic, last-minute antics, marathon sessions, or procrastination.

Unhealthy groups are:

- **Perfection obsessed**—Fearing that their best will not be good enough, they prepare for every contingency and for every decision to fail.

- **Dependent or Codependent**—They either look for someone to rescue them or become themselves the saviors of the church. Often one person will end up doing all the work, thus becoming indispensable.

- **Boundary-less**—Some committees drive their pastors crazy because they are constantly passing legislation that disturbs or disrupts what another group is trying to do. Other committees meet and meet but fail to do anything because they haven't yet discovered their area of responsibility or purpose.

- **Time-Stressed**—Groups that have lost their way will often require their members to make unreasonable time commitments.

Leaders should shift their leadership styles depending upon how healthy they perceive each committee, or the entire church organization, to be. Furthermore, the effective leader guides the pace of group discussion, ensuring that the group is not slowed by its perfectionism or rushed into a codependent relationship. When a group is healthy, it views time as a resource which it can faithfully manage.

Healing leaders constantly communicate their appreciation for the willingness of the group's members to work together. They emphasize that together they are a team. Healing leaders also remind groups that if they have followed a good process, they will learn from their mistakes and, in the end, have a better track record than they would have had if they had striven to be perfect or listened to their anxieties. As time goes on, the group members will grow in trust of each other and gain confidence in their collective wisdom. God does not call church committees to be perfect; God calls them to be faithful. No matter how religious they pretend to be, they will not behave faithfully if anxiety rules.

Groups gel and become more effective when they discover how to speak about their anxieties and still make decisions.

Another challenge for the healing leader is getting the task-oriented members of the group at least to notice the concerns of the relationship-oriented people of the group. The leader also helps relationship-oriented people to understand the importance of achieving some tasks. Doing this may involve helping people name and claim their own personality type or temperament. The healing leader spends time at each meeting stating appreciation for the gifts each individual brings to the table. The leader specifically complements those whom the rest of the group may undervalue. Every congregation has in its collective memory stories of when a person of low prestige provided the missing ingredient and "saved the day." Recount these narratives in those anxious times to guide the group away from looking for a knight in shining armor (or the "perfect pastor") to ride in and tell them what to do.

To be this type of leader for a group or a congregation requires a great deal of role clarity. As I go from meeting to meeting in my various roles as a pastor and conference staffperson, I often ask myself, "What role am I to play here?" If the group is working together with discernment, reason, and wisdom, then I try to bring my own gifts to the mix and seek simply to be one of the team. But if anxiety is preventing the group from meshing, I ask myself what needs to be done to restore effective group process. *Can I model a non-anxious presence for this group, or have things reached the point where we need to bring in an outsider?* From time to time, it is healthy for committees to invite an outside person with known healing gifts to participate with them for several meetings. If there is only a moderate level of anxiety, then someone in the group may be able to act as the non-anxious presence. But if the group process has become totally compromised, it will be hard for participants to set aside their own anxieties. Clergy, in particular, need to be aware of their own limitations in the healing process. Groups should not hesitate to bring in someone from the outside. When congregations are part of a cluster or cooperative ministry, they have the option of lending healing leaders back and forth. Adjacent clergy and social workers with a specialty in family-systems work may also have the necessary skills to coach committees and congregations regarding their group dynamics. Churches should be willing to look not only to their own denominational offices, but also to ecumenical organizations with a track record in resolving church conflict.

BETWEEN PASTORS

Interim or transitional ministers are a special form of non-anxious leaders. They come into situations where the congregation's anxiety over the pastoral change needs to heal before the church can return to productivity. Since they have this very specific, clearly-defined role, they guide the group through a series of developmental tasks. After six to twenty-four months, they move on, leaving behind a healthier congregation. These developmental tasks are very similar to the points that Shakespeare's Marc Anthony makes in his funeral oration. The tasks are:

- Accepting Past History;
- Clarifying the Congregation's Mission and Identity;
- Allowing Needed Leadership Change;
- Reconnecting with the Denomination;
- Becoming Committed to Doing New Things.

In most mainline denominations, the change of clergy from one congregation to another is a well-thought-out, highly-structured, competently-managed process—except for those times when it isn't. The bishops and district superintendents that I know in the United Methodist Church take pride in the way our system reduces congregational anxiety by providing new pastoral leadership within the very same week that the old leadership departs. Since both clergy and congregations have been carefully instructed on how to maintain momentum through pastoral transitions, you would expect that each change would bring fresh ideas and release the congregation for new missional activity. I estimate that about a third of these transitions are not normal. The first task of the new clergy is to address and neutralize congregational anxiety.

Consider the following:

- An over-functioning, codependent, or manipulative clergy has asserted his or her authority in almost every aspect of church life. People ask, "How can we survive without Pastor Smith? He always told us what to do." Anxiety will be high in the church until the laity learn how to function in their roles.

- Pastor Jones, after eight years at Gentle Valley UMC, has retired. Her real retirement, however, took place somewhere in the middle of her tenure when she began counting the days until she was sixty-two. Some of the congregation express their anxiety by complaining that the new, young pastor doesn't do home visitation. The real anxiety, which goes unsaid, is that the congregation may already have lost the younger folk who would appreciate the new programs that this pastor wants to start.

- The Old Crossroads Church is anxious during this pastoral appointment season because their finances have reached the point where they need to become a two-point circuit. They hope this will not mean giving up their 11 AM worship time, but the district superintendent hasn't made any promises. This anxiety is heightened by the fact that it is now mid-May, and they won't have much courting time to get to know the other church, which will soon be sharing their pastor. Meanwhile, a little distance away, a clergy family is wondering how they are going to adjust to the added work stress the proposed charge arrangement will bring.

I am convinced that much of the long-term conflict that we see in churches today has its origin in poorly managed transition. Anxiety is like the water from a leaky upstairs plumbing fixture. The spot where it shows up on the first floor ceiling may be some distance from where the pipes are leaking. Anxiety travels in the hidden murmurings of a congregation for a long time. When it erupts in conflict, our first reaction is to blame the persons and issues immediately involved. Fixing the ceiling doesn't solve the problem of the leaky plumbing. Adhering to an appropriate transitional process allows for the real issues to surface and for healing to take place.

TERMINAL ANXIETY

Churches also become anxious when they have to dismiss a staffperson or request a change of clergy. We need to remember that most members of our congregation have never been in a position to terminate someone's employment. I had been in pastoral ministry for nearly twenty years before I had my first experience with having to fire an employee. I then found myself delivering the "We appreciate your years of service but we must now let you go . . ." speech, twice in the same year. As I reflect on my feelings and the deliberations of the staffing committee, I see two distinct sources of anxiety, the task-oriented anxiety about whether we were doing the right thing and the relational anxiety about what effect this action would have on the person we fired. Sometimes these concerns and the people who voice them conflict. An employee may be doing a wonderful job and be hard to replace, but their relational skills are so poor that they have failed to become part of the staff team. A member of the pastoral-relations committee may say, "I know Joe will land like a cat on his feet after we let him go, but he's also likely to trash our reputation and leave us struggling to replace him." An organist may have played faithfully for forty years. Everyone on the committee grieves for the hurt she will feel if they force her into retirement. "It may kill her," someone remarks. "But," the pastor says, "We are dying as a congregation. We scare away first-time attenders each time Bernice falters in the prelude or stumbles through a contemporary praise song."

One of the leader's tasks in these situations is to recognize the presence of anxiety and ensure that both sides, the task-oriented and the relationship-oriented, voice their concerns. It may well be that the group lacks clarity about whether they are making the right decision. Should they schedule another meeting and covenant to spend time in prayerful discernment? Or the group may have reached consensus about the need to terminate, and it now needs to deal with the delicate matter of fashioning a healthy exit strategy for the employee. The group also needs to discuss how and when they will communicate their decision to the rest of the congregation.

Often, staffing committees fail to consider their roles as communicators. They need to discuss when and how others will hear of their decisions. There is a difference between confidentiality and secrecy. Secrecy involves the hiding of information in order to gain an advantage or to maintain one's power in a situation. Secrecy is never appropriate in a church. Its presence indicates that the congregation has a relationship-oriented culture with accompanying systemic dysfunctions (discussed in chapter three). Confidentiality, on the other hand, involves protecting the rights of people to choose if and how they will disclose personal information. Something as innocuous as a middle name may be kept confidential if the person requests it. Obviously, security issues, such as an employee's social-security number, need to be kept confidential. The reprimands that an employee has received from their supervisors should be kept in a locked file with the committee members taking responsibility for keeping that information confidential. The employee chooses whom he or she will talk to about any job-related stress. No one outside of the appropriate decision-making process has the right to know that an employee will be terminated before that employee is told. Once a termination occurs, the employee may be invited to share feelings about when and how the congregation should be told. The committee, however, must take responsibility for communicating this news to the congregation. Confidentiality and compassion for the exiting employee often means the committee must share that they made this decision, but they are not at liberty to explain the details or the incidences that led to the termination. Confidentiality may sound like secrecy, but it never serves the personal needs of the committee, and it always protects the rights of the employee to tell his or her own story.

Clergy should be aware that how they train their pastoral-relations committee to behave in regards to other staff will be the model for how the committee will treat them. Each year this committee receives new members, and each year the senior pastor must take the time to explain the meaning of confidentiality. Furthermore, the wise pastor cultivates diversity and open discussion in this committee and in other administrative groups. It is important for individuals to express minority viewpoints during the meetings. Even when the group does not achieve consensus, people should trust the process enough to buy into and support the group's decision. When the day comes that the group has to make a decision that affects the pastor personally, he or she will be glad that group members have taken the time to develop healthy group process. Pastoral committees should meet at least monthly during the first year after a pastoral change and bi-monthly after that. In multiple-point situations, the pastoral-relations committee often functions as a unifying body for the charge. They need to meet more frequently simply to keep the pastor from becoming fragmented. The members of this critical group need to know how to trust each other with integrity and unity before they speak about difficult matters concerning the key leadership of the congregation.

Stress

Congregational stress is similar to congregational anxiety. Something in the sermon sparks a controversy between the pastor and an anonymous letter writer. George, who knows nothing of the letters, notices the edge in Pastor Judy's voice and asks her if she is under stress. The trustees meet late into the night as they ponder a leaky roof, a wheezing organ, and an option to purchase the lot next door. It is helpful to remember that the word "stress" is an engineering term that describes two similar conditions. What I call "polarity stress" happens when there is a tension between two values, options, or parties. The individual, group, or congregation experiencing polarity stress feels as if opposing forces are straining a rope to the breaking point. By way of contrast, "overload stress" is the state of trying to deal with too much stuff too short quickly or with limited organizational resources. The Hebrew slaves in Egypt experienced this kind of stress when Pharaoh required them to make the same quota of bricks while gathering their own straw (Exodus 5:6-21). When groups downsize while maintaining the same expectations, they frequently experience overload stress. Both forms of stress, like anxiety, hamper a group's ability to behave as compassionate, reflective, and spiritual people responding appropriately to their context. Like a cable stretched beyond its limits or a bag filled too full, the first visible sign of a stress problem may be the catastrophic destruction of the organization. As we pick up the pieces of a church in conflict, we often note with shock the amount of emotional stress present within the congregational system.

Anxiety tends to expand a person's sense of time. Anxious people will wax historic as they tell their tales, drawing in events that happened decades ago and speaking about them as if they happened yesterday. Stress, on the other hand, compresses our experience of time. We see only what is immediately before us. When the overloaded shelf breaks, our response is to blame the shelf or the most recent item placed upon it rather than to reflect upon the variety of items that we loaded onto it over time. When a conflict breaks out over an issue of substance, anxiety results in a polarized congregation, dividing it into camps for or against an item. Polarizing stress tends to cause tunnel vision, limiting the debate to one aspect of the conflict. Pastor Jack obsesses about the one line of his sermon quoted in the letters, rather than reflecting upon this congregation's history of submerging controversy and dealing with relational issues in secret. The stressed-out person cannot see the forest for the trees. The stressed-out congregation forgets its heritage and forsakes its current members in an attempt to manage the current crisis.

When the stress level is too high, the wise leader looks for ways to help those around him or her gain perspective. This move feels counterintuitive. We tend to want to reduce stress by increasing efficiency. In order to accomplish more at church-council meetings, a stress-enhancing chair will both forgo the reading of the minutes and shortchange the opening devotions. The leader who is aware of the nature of stress, however, intentionally uses prayer and scriptural reflections to set the current crisis within the context of God's providence. In times of stress, organizations need to reexamine their mission and vision statements so they act with a mind to the future. They may need to scan back over years of minutes to see how they resolved similar issues. The stress-aware leader will manage the pace of discussions and schedule separate meetings to develop strategic vision. Stress accentuates the need to make quick tactical decisions; church committees caught up in its fury often will win the battle while losing the war.

In thinking about polarity stress, it is helpful to reflect on the many ways in which tension is useful in our world. Suspension bridges utilize tension to support our roads, springs under tension keep our doors closed, and the competitive tension between differing brands on the market keeps prices reasonable. When polarities arise in the church, our first temptation may be to defuse the conflict by ignoring one side or excluding its views from consideration. A pastor caught in a scheduling conflict between a family commitment and a church event may choose to ignore the family's prior request of his or her time. Or the pastor may state, "Family is always my first priority" and fail to consider that this particular event has significance for the long-term effectiveness of the church. Black-and-white thinking, or the immediate jumping to one side of a polarity, is a sure sign that an individual or group has succumbed to the insanity of stress. Congregations and leaders who have learned the wisdom of keeping spiritually focused while living in a stress-filled world practice the art of keeping issues in tension. They see it as normal that the parsonage family and the church family will have conflicting plans for particular blocks of the pastor's time. The congregation needs to realize that there will be similar tensions between groups that want to use the same rooms at the same time. If the church has both a traditional and a contemporary service, it is normal to experience ongoing stress between the two. Instead of seeking to resolve this tension with a one-time absolute decision or a set of hard-andp-fast rules, all parties need to recognize that a polarity exists. Polarities are managed, not eliminated. Managing a polarity means constantly revisiting the issue. It means allowing both parties to express their needs, seeking "win-win" solutions when possible, and making balanced compromises when choices must be made. It also means recognizing that all decisions are human, fallible, and less than perfect. Instead of seeking to be right, the leader caught in the middle of polarity stress must seek to be transparent, compassionate, and true to the values that people on both sides of the issue hold in common.

Congregations seem to have a particularly hard time viewing theological polarities as normal and healthy. There is a common misconception that anyone who is "Christian" will read the Bible in a particular way, maintain that certain human behavior is sinful, and support prescribed political causes. Very few people in the church today understand theological interpretation as an ongoing process. Fewer still are willing to recognize that complex and difficult issues, by their nature, generate a range of responses. There is instead an expectation that the denomination, or the pastor, or the church board must provide simple litmus tests as to who is in and who is out. The best that church leadership can do, however, is to draw fuzzy boundaries around an acceptable range of thought. As the church deals with "hot" issues, it is constantly redefining what we, as a collective body, believe. If we keep the dialogue open, both those to the right and to the left of center can make honest contributions. Systems tend to be self-regulating. If a church seeks to become more conservative by ousting those it deems too liberal, eventually it will find that some of its formerly centrist members have now drifted to the left to take the place of the departed ones.

Jesus ministered to a people who were highly polarized between those who accepted the Roman occupation of Palestine and those who advocated armed insurrection. Some of Jesus' most memorable statements honored this tension while pointing to a more loving way of living. He said to turn the other cheek and to give unto Caesar that which is Caesar's.

All of this is to say that those who hope to create unity in the church by limiting what they permit people to believe, do, or politically support are pursuing a fruitless and possibly dangerous fiction. When we expect diversity and allow polarities to exist in tension, we encourage our membership to view each other and the neighbors outside the church as people. Allowing theological and ethical polarities to exist in tension pushes us to find deeper shared truths and values on which to base our unity.

OVERLOAD STRESS AND DEPRESSION

Congregations can also face overload stress, a condition marked by having too much to do with too few resources. Unfortunately, among American churches, over-commitment rarely causes this condition. It is possible for a congregation to overload because compassion has driven them to attempt to do more good in the world (mission) than they have resources to do. A church just inland from a hurricane-disaster zone may feel overwhelmed as it ministers to those who have lost their homes. I know of a small congregation with only a few adult leaders, and yet they have responded to the latchkey kids of their neighborhood with a variety of programs. Looking out over the two dozen squirming kids gathered for the summer lunch program, one volunteer said to the other, "I'm getting too old for this." To which the other replied, "But don't you know when you look in their faces that God is good!"

Overload stress can also occur in a task-oriented congregation led by a manipulative pastor. Some leaders have a wealth of "driven-ness" and know how to drive the people around them beyond all reasonable limits. The church might be gearing up for a stewardship drive to support a major building project, but the pastor is busily pushing for an expansion in mission support. The church council may have ten items on its agenda, but the pastor begs the chairperson to add two more items that are urgent and to permit a vendor to make a half-hour presentation at the beginning of the meeting. The church leadership splits between needing to ramp up the new worship service and the pastor's plan to reformat the church's christian education around a new small-group concept. When people complain about all the church meetings they have to attend to make these things happen, the pastor chastises them for not being fully committed. Overload stress, especially when instigated by an over-achieving pastor, always exacts its price. Leaders may complete the activities and projects, but the good people who sacrificed to make them happen reach a state of burnout and begin to search for ways to drop out. There is a gradual loss of people until the pastor announces that he or she has been appointed or called elsewhere. While this type of driven leadership is often rewarded for achievements, it leaves behind three casualties:

- The congregation has been taught to depend upon the pastor to tell them what to do. They no longer own their own vision, values, or sense of identity.

- The transition to the next pastor is usually chaotic. People are anxious to see this new pastor juggle all the balls that the previous pastor put in the air.

- The self-esteem of the congregation has been wounded. They now believe that they are incapable of supporting the vision of a great pastor.

By far, the most common cause of overload stress today is congregational decline and aging. Consider the case of a beautiful and conflicted church on the main street of a small Pennsylvania town. This church had over seven hundred members in 1985, but by century's end was down to four hundred on the rolls and under one hundred in active worship participation. This decline continued into the new millennium in spite of the fact that they had successfully started a contemporary worship service and had a well-maintained, handicap-accessible building with plenty of parking. It would be easy to blame the pastoral leadership; the church has had three pastors in twelve years, two of whom were essentially run out of town by factions in the congregation. These same pastors went on to lead thriving congregations elsewhere. As I did the history on this church, I found myself wondering how such nice people could be so nasty to their clergy. Looking at the situation in context, however, I noticed that the last two decades were a time of continuous reductions in the workforce at the town's principal employer. The families of blue-collar workers who took pride in their town and local industry had once led the church. Today, its leadership consisted entirely of retirees; cutbacks had forced them to leave the mill before they had planned. As young people exited the town, the church had an exodus of energy, even though they managed to stay afloat financially by using their endowments and bequests. This enabled them to hire talented preachers. They expected these pastors to make them feel good about a bad situation. When they failed, the congregation's leadership became expert at giving them the boot.

Depression, whatever its cause, leads inevitably to conflict. As it becomes harder and harder to achieve results that were easy in the past, overload stress becomes the elephant in the room that no one talks about. Congregational depression leads to denial, anger, and the search for simplistic solutions or easy scapegoats. This loss of perspective prevents church leadership from doing the necessary reassessment of their mission and context. Stress is not the product of having too much to do with too few resources; it is instead the natural consequence of failing to adjust to current reality. The arrival of a new, visionary leader cannot cure this malaise. Rather the church needs talk therapy. The church needs to celebrate its history, while at the same time letting go of expectations that the present will be like the past. It needs to empower its current leadership, lay and clergy, to work with the strengths and opportunities the church has today.

Depressed congregations tend to focus on survival. They struggle to maintain half-empty buildings, as well as organizational structures, staffing, and various programs, as if they believe these things are sacred in themselves (see *Saul's Armor*, Discipleship Resources 2007). There is a certain threadbare bagginess to these once-proud churches. They are like the person who has lost a lot of weight but fails to buy new clothes to fit his or her new size. As churches decline, they should engage in a process of discernment with the goal of changing their organizational structure to suit their mission for today. If they no longer have the need for a full-time ordained pastor (generally 125 in worship attendance) or the programs to justify staff, they should get off that treadmill and seek other ways of being in ministry. They need to rediscover the wisdom of the ancient words, "To every thing there is a season . . ." (Ecclesiastes 3:1 KJV).

There are five rules for dealing with congregational depression:

1) **Focus on being rather than doing:** The congregation does not need a set of goals to help them feel guilty. They need pastoral sermons on the art of being the people of God.

They need a church council that desires to be Christ-like in their process and their actions. They need mission activities and programs that allow them to feel good while doing good (people oriented instead of project oriented).

2) **Visit the past but return to the present:** Tradition is meant to form our values and identity but not to determine our future. Have people talk about their history, but guide them to recognize how the present context is irreversibly different from the past. Redefine what it means to be successful as a congregation.

3) **Celebrate simple Christianity:** Allow people to realize that all who follow Jesus Christ proclaim the great truths of the faith. Encourage all the people of God to seek the renewing power of God's Spirit.

4) **Don't try to be what you currently aren't:** Allow for graceful downsizing. Replace staff with volunteers. Train people to use their spiritual gifts. Orient the church's expectations toward those things that you have the skills and resources to accomplish.

5) **Manage your transitions well:** Each time a change of leadership is necessary, think about how to manage the transition. What can you do to honor the outgoing person? How will you permit the new leader to redefine the role and use his or her unique gifts? What can you do to encourage each church leader to mentor replacements and to make rotation of leadership a normal function of this church?

Receptivity to Change

Recently, I arrived late at night and bone tired at my local airport. Having faced more than the usual travel delays and stress, I wondered if I had sufficient caffeine in my system to drive the hour home to my bed. A few miles down the highway, I encountered the orange and white barrels that told me that the long-talked-about repair to the parkway had begun. Suddenly a "road closed" detour sign put me off my familiar route and into an unfamiliar neighborhood. Soon I was helplessly lost. I am convinced that this lostness would not have occurred if I had been less tired, if there had been daylight, and if the detour signs had been more informative. Because of my fatigue, I was not very receptive to the changes the highway department had made that night. Yet, I consider myself a person who loves change.

Congregations will appear opposed to change when in fact they are stressed, anxious, or the victims of poor communication. Both as individuals and as groups, people utilize three different modes for responding to life's detours. While individual habits or the culture of an organization may predispose it towards one particular mode, every entity has the capability of choosing how it will respond to change.

REACTIVE MODE

This defensive mode assumes a zero-sum game; it gains nothing. The reactive person or congregation believes there must be a "loser" in the competition of old versus new and that they have no choice but to stick with the old, even though it may be the losing side of the game. A small-membership church may view the new mega-church in its neighborhood as an intruder and may say, "They get all their people by stealing our members." Just as I was unwilling to accept that the workers were actually improving the highway to the airport for my eventual benefit, the reactive congregation isn't able to admit that new churches and forms of ministry and evangelism are actually winning new people to Christ. Because reactivity is by nature competitive and exclusive, it is often coupled with narrow worldviews. Reactive organizations behave like trapped animals: they become angry, flail about and sometimes hurt innocent individuals, and engage in manipulative behaviors to try to keep change from happening.

When people become habitually reactive, it is a mistake to label them averse to change. People who are reactive in one area of life may be progressive in another. They may be the first to adopt the latest technology in the workplace but at home may throw a fit because someone has slightly moved the furniture. In a similar way, a progressive, newly-formed church may respond reactively to a minor change in their ministerial staffing. They may sign off on a multimillion-dollar mortgage with hardly any debate but balk at the associate minister taking a study leave. With individuals, as well as congregational systems, it pays to evaluate the level of anxiety and stress that was present before the stimuli took place. What hides in the individual or congregation's history that causes them to react explosively to this particular issue? It may not be possible to learn the exact problem, but I suggest that compassion must become a part of the approach to change.

To move away from reactive behavior, organizations and individuals need to know they are secure. The instinctive physiological response ("fight or flight") locks individuals into reactivity when they feel threatened by a change in environment. A person's adrenalin-laden blood chemistry needs calm to release anxiety and to diminish the effects of stress. In a similar fashion, anxiety can saturate congregations when messages that focus on church survival charge relational networks. Until people recognize that their cherished traditions and institutions are not in danger, they will move into some form of irrational thought or behavior. The city clerk of Ephesus realized this when the artisans of his city rioted over the preaching of the Apostle Paul in Acts 19:23-41. Rather than wading in with rational arguments concerning the merits of Paul's theology, the clerk calmed the crowds by telling them their traditional work was still secure. I suspect, though I have no evidence to support this, that an economic downturn in the silversmith craft set the stage for the reactive atmosphere that greeted Paul's preaching that day.

The city clerk played the role of a non-anxious leader. In the church, non-anxious pastors help their congregations rediscover the sense of personal and corporate security that faith can provide believers. In spite of the current crisis, the church is still of God and will continue to have a role to play in bringing healing to the people of this particular congregation's context. Reactive people need to hear that they are already "children of God" (1 John 3:2). Note how Jesus begins the Sermon on the Mount (Matthew 5:2-12) with an assurance that those gathered are already blessed. His message would radically challenge their religious practice and personal lifestyle. Knowing that God was already with them prepared this early congregation to respond positively to the kingdom of God and the changes it would involve. This is a counterintuitive approach for helping people to become risk-takers. Instead of preaching a sermon concerning how much people will have to change, Jesus blesses them with insights into how the kingdom of God is already among them. Instead of prescribing a list of actions they must perform, Jesus helps the people recover the basic values that inform all genuine religious behavior. As church leaders, our first impulse is to prescribe action, when the healing rightly comes from a focus upon who we are and what we may become. Any suggestion that there is a right or a wrong way to meet the challenge of change only polarizes people more deeply into their competitive positions. The therapeutic church leader helps people recognize the sources of their anxiety and stress and then equips them to behave according to the values learned through the grace of God. Once people can name their fears, they usually are on the road toward discovering new ways to adapt to change and to discover creative "win-win" solutions for living with others.

RESPONSIVE MODE

Mature individuals hope to respond rather than react to change. I could have responded to my unexpected detour by pulling off to the side of the road and consulting a map or stopping for directions. Instead of focusing upon my desire to get home and to bed, I could have slowed down and carefully paid attention to the detour signs.

Responsive behavior involves checking our prior assumptions against current reality. We intentionally gather additional information and slow down our processes until we are certain of our choices. To the outsider, an organization that is responding appropriately to change may appear conservative. The responsive church is not the first congregation in the area to accept or invest in a new program. The responsive church is clear about values and mission but flexible about the tactics it needs to achieve a positive outcome in the midst of change. Because this church has an optimistic "God remains in charge" theology, the responsive church willingly accepts the existence of change and seeks intelligent responses.

The responsive mode is a "look before you leap" approach to change. As the neighborhood around the church changes, responsive church leaders track the demographics and seek new ways to meet the needs of those who live nearby. For the responsive church leadership, every activity of the church is on the table for discussion and possible change. Leaders will discuss, without becoming reactive, the number of services and the style of worship the church will offer. The core values of the congregation and its mission to proclaim God's love, however, are nonnegotiable. Congregations can be responsive to change as long as they are secure in their own sense of identity, trust their current clergy leadership, and maintain a healthy optimism about the future. Pull one of these essential attitudes out of the mix and even the most hope-filled people become averse to risk, inflexible, and reactive. In the church, anxiety and agility are mutually exclusive.

PROACTIVE MODE

When I told others of my midnight detour, they wondered why I hadn't paid attention to the frequent notifications the road department had issued regarding the project. I could have been proactive and planned an alternate route. In spite of being constantly admonished to "think ahead," congregations and individuals very rarely behave proactively. Proactive people tend to exhibit an entrepreneurial spirit that anticipates with and rejoices in the opportunities that change brings. The proactive road warrior rejoices in the opportunity to use global positioning systems to discover new ways of getting there. If life gives them lemons, they make lemonade. Rather than waiting for change to run over them, they intentionally look over the horizon to glimpse what is coming. They are optimistic about their own abilities to work for their advantage, whatever the future brings. Proactive cultures tend to develop in organizations that value continuous improvement. This is what I refer to as "agility." It is the ability to set short goals continuously and then muster all of one's resources to meet that challenge. (I address this in *Saul's Armor*, part of the Congregational Leaders Empowered for Change series.)

Besides a low level of anxiety and an optimistic attitude towards the future, congregations that behave proactively display an ability to view the world from alternate points of view. For example, Washington Church was organized in 1774 as a vital witness in the community. Its leadership continues to seek ways to understand how newcomers will view their neighborhood. Instead of reactively complaining about the loss of members to the region's mega-church, a proactive congregation may seek creatively to understand how to attract new residents who prefer the intimate fellowship of a small-membership church. They then target an advertisement campaign to reach this demographic.

One of the first casualties of high anxiety is the ability to think creatively. People with a crisis mindset have a difficult time seeing their problems, let alone their context, from other points of view.

Back to David and Saul

How much anxiety and stress were present in the total social system when David played his harp for Saul? In his youth, Saul was known for his military victories. His skills as a warrior bolstered the Israelite economy and helped define the new nation as a regional power. His charismatic style of leadership served him well as the first king of Israel, but Saul lacked the managerial skills to develop a stable monarchy. At the end of his reign, the Philistines again threatened to enslave Israel. Then the prophet Samuel died. Samuel had been both a spiritual leader and a unifying presence in the nation. While Saul may have had his differences with Samuel, he needed the old man. Things then fell apart, not only because Saul exhibited manic-depressive traits, but also because the social system was in transition and needed a transitional leader.

Transitional times are inherently anxious and stressful. This chapter sets forth an alternative view of conflict. We often assume that church fights are the fault of irrational people or the unavoidable byproduct of irreconcilable differences of opinion. I believe that conflict is the icing on whatever cultural cake the congregation has baked out of its emotional journey. The flavor of the cake may be very different from the flavor of the icing. The behavior of any congregation during times of high anxiety will differ from its normal behavior. When you dig back into the history of a congregation, you may notice characteristic behavior reoccurring during each period of crisis. Old First may fire their secretary or janitor each time they become overstressed. The people over at Grace Church may express their anxiety by taking an extreme stance on a current social issue. Instead of chasing these diversions, I have learned to ask the deeper question related to the purpose of the church, which I hope that you will also ask: "What systemic work does the congregation need to accomplish during this time of upheaval?" or "What will it take for the people of this church to feel secure again?" Each transitional process has a different set of goals that it needs to achieve. One congregation may need to establish limits on its lay leadership; another may need to develop financial controls to restore the confidence of the people. A third church may need to learn to cope with diverse social or political opinions.

When David succeeded Saul, several years of civil war also followed because the transitional process happened within the context of a competition between two military leaders. People wanted to see a confrontation, if for no other reason than to prove they had backed the stronger leader. David, however, kept on restating the transitional process in other, less competitive terms. While Saul was alive, David had many supporters who boasted that he had killed more Philistines than Saul. David never gloried in this statistic. Instead, he reminded people that Saul was the Lord's anointed. This preserved the authority of the king's office, so that the people could one day understand and respect David as the Lord's anointed. When Saul died, David realized he had a new transitional task in melding the various tribes into one nation. To accomplish this goal, David moved the seat of government and worship to the neutral city of Jerusalem. His clarity about the transitional task provides a fitting example for any clergyperson who attempts to lead a congregation through transition.

Like David we often inherit a conflict midstream. The exiting pastor may have used talents or charm to create a loyal following. Now the congregation is poised to turn the transition into a popularity contest. Paul experienced this in Corinth when he heard different factions in the church proclaim, "'I belong to Apollos,' or 'I belong to Cephas' . . ." (I Corinthians 1:12). The incoming pastor needs to restate patiently the real goal of the transition, which is to have a healthy relationship between pastor and parish for the purpose of making disciples for Jesus Christ.

Learning to be a non-anxious church leader is the universal tool for meeting a variety of conflict situations. Take time to discover the forms of stress and anxiety that are weakening your church. Mine congregational history for clues to understand the current cultural climate. Take nothing for granted or at face value during a transition.

Application Points

These questions will allow you to review the main points of this chapter. Working through this chapter and these points with other church leaders may provide for meaningful conversation about ministry and purpose.

1) How does your congregation rotate leadership? Think about the organizational structure of your church by examining the following:

- Does your denomination require specific term limits? Do you apply these term limits appropriately?

- Has the church council adopted additional guidelines for leadership rotation and leadership training? How do people move in and out of leadership and from position to position?

How does the church discern individual gifts and availability for service?

2) How would you rate the overall congregational anxiety level?

Cool as a cucumber:
(Low Anxiety)   0 ... 1 ... 2 ... 3 ... 4 ... 5   (High Anxiety)

3) What forms of stress are currently present in your congregation?

Polarity Stress: (name examples)

Overload Stress: (name examples)

4) How would you rate your non-defensive listening skills? Take time to assess one another on the leadership team.

5) What can you do to improve your skills as a non-anxious leader? Who can offer honest feedback about your skills?

6) How has the congregation handled the last three pastoral changes? Is the current anxiety level on the rise in anticipation of a future pastoral change? What can the congregation do now to prepare for a smoother transition?

CHAPTER TWO

Quadrant One: The Culture of Task Orientation

All I Really Need to Know I Learned in Kindergarten

Robert Fulghum

So the king [Solomon] said, "Bring me a sword," and they brought a sword before the king. The King said, "Divide the living boy in two; then give half to one [woman] and half to the other [woman]."

I Kings 3:24-25

From time to time a committee or group, such as the trustees or the women's fellowship, will become overly task-oriented. They zealously weed out of their meetings any chitchat or idle inquiry about one another's well being. They focus their agendas on the steady accomplishment of objectives. They want results, but in the process, they lose sight of the dual nature of the kingdom of God. God's kingdom ministers to the people engaged in its mission just as much as it transforms the world. Sometimes this culture of task orientation spreads to the whole organization. Overly task-oriented groups also sometimes teach new church leaders to render crisp reports and assume that nothing happens at a meeting that they cannot record in the minutes. They reduce the complex, interpersonal network of a living congregation to a sterile organizational chart. These types of groups and congregations often fall prey to substantial conflicts. They argue over facts, over building projects, and over which course of action demonstrates the best stewardship of resources. They are also prone to turf wars and, even worse, to endless debate over who was supposed to handle what item of business, where in the budget an expense item belongs, or what the proper policy or procedure should be in every situation.

You may expect this culture to occur only in those rare congregations made up exclusively of accountants and CEOs. Not so! One can find substantial conflict and the task-oriented culture that it thrives on throughout the church. There may be theological roots for this in the Protestant roots of John Wesley and John Calvin, but I think the real cause is the spirit of perfectionism that dominated American culture in the mid-part of the twentieth century. Post-modernism is ending the reign of perfectionism, or at least changing its form. A majority of people born after 1947 expect that their church work will take place within a team context. They want to be both holistically affirmed as individuals and integrated into a complex social web. Local churches, however, are frequently behind the times. Further, becoming excessively task-oriented or shutting down as if in shock is a common organizational response to major trauma. Please note this special form of trauma: Just as an individual reared with abuse will often appear emotionally flat and disinclined to engage in relational bantering, so also will a congregation that has experienced clergy misconduct retreat into a businesslike approach to all of its work.

Small-membership churches as a whole tend to be highly relational. Sometimes one encounters a church in which a layer of task orientation seems imposed on top of an otherwise relational culture. Digging down through the layers of the congregation's history, one encounters stories in which a pastor or other key leaders betrayed the congregation's trust.

In order to avoid more pain, the people have adopted a prescribed set of procedures and policies to protect the institution from harm and offer a shield against potential vulnerability. To focus solely on the agenda and its objectives limits emotional vulnerability. It also creates a protective barrier around personal relationships in the congregation so that outsiders (such as the pastor) cannot damage them again.

Substantial conflicts also occur in otherwise healthy churches. A county-seat congregation in the Midwest finds itself divided over whether to retain its liberal pastor. The task-oriented lay leader wants to take a survey or a congregational vote to solve what appears to him to be a simple "yes or no" proposition. A suburban church receives a proposal to rent its facilities to a secular daycare operation. The trustees alone make a decision and sign the agreement. The many complaints from individuals and groups in the church surprise the trustees. Conflicts in these relationally cold climates may seem to be soley about the issues and thus easily solved by reason. Yet failure to deal with the relational aspects of these differences of opinion may create lasting animosity, alienate otherwise supportive members, and force the exit of angry or hurt leaders, whether lay or ordained.

Churches that reside in task-oriented quadrant one are prone to discount the importance of broad communication. Their leaders think it is inappropriate to bounce ideas off the folks in the pew before leaders make a decision. These leaders feel they hold a church office because of their ideas or their capacity to act. They rarely consider the fact that they may be in this position because people trust them as individuals of faith within the congregation and that their greatest contribution may be to pray and discern the will of the body and the will of God. For them, the nature and purpose of the church is solely its activity, its mission. These leaders are perplexed by those who speak about the church as a fellowship of diverse people. Because of this blind spot, these quadrant-one leaders often fail to take the time to develop grassroots support for their projects. When an opposition party materializes, it shocks quadrant-one leaders when people become unreasonable. Only then do these leaders begin to look for tools to deal with substantial conflict.

Tools for Substantial Conflict

As Robert Fulghum notes, most of us learned the essential tools for conflict resolution while we were in kindergarten. When people have different objectives for the church or when issues divide us, we simply need to think of ourselves as children on a playground and utilize the appropriate decision-making process. While it may seem counterintuitive, leaders within a task-oriented culture should learn that the way they facilitate making decisions in the church is more important than the outcome. Everything creates precedents and builds a pattern for the resolution of future issues. When the method of making decisions stifles creativity or ignores aspects of fellowship within the community of Christ, we are setting the stage for organizational stagnation, and we will eventually discover irreconcilable differences.

A variety of tools from kindergarten helps to resolve substantial conflicts or differences of opinion. The simplest aids involve flipping a coin, picking straws, or playing a round of rock-paper-scissors. Sometimes these very simple methods are not helpful. We run into problems when the core issue does not concern what to do, but how we relate to one another. Conflicts are often like icebergs, with a visible component revealing substance and the larger, more dangerous, and hidden part concerned with relationships. Church leaders also run into difficulty when they have only a limited number of tools or problem-solving approaches, or when they have a favorite methodology that they use exclusively and perhaps inappropriately. In I Kings 3, Solomon showed himself to be a wise fool by applying an unusual tool of mediation in a situation where he was the arbiter. Consider each of the following tools and their limitations.

HIGHER ARBITRATION

When we discover two children fighting over the same toy, we may intercede by declaring, "The toy belongs to Sam because it was his birthday present." This declaration resolves conflict by applying the tool of higher arbitration. We act as a judge, determining the case by weighing the merit each child has on his or her side of the argument. This tool works well in many cases, feels fair (at least to the arbitrator or parent), and often results in an easily implemented plan (give the toy to Sam). Higher arbitration, however, assumes that the issue or item being fought over is indivisible and that winner must take all. Once one pulls this method out of the toolbox, it also becomes hard to invite people to discuss the possibility of compromise. The participants in conflict may not notice the dynamic aspects of this win-loose process, but neutral observers notice and comment.

In I Kings 3, once the two women arguing over the baby decided to go to King Solomon for arbitration, neither showed any interest in joint custody. Often, a group in the church will disagree with the pastor over a substantial issue. As long as the dialogue occurs within the congregation, it is possible that someone will design a win-win compromise, or that those engaged in the disagreement will accept the wisdom of a larger gathering of the congregation. Such a situation, however, quickly polarizes (only one side can win) when one person decides to complain to a judicatory leader or invites a judicatory leader to make a judgment in the case. This outside person becomes the designated higher arbitrator. In several situations, a judicatory leader may come to the church to hear presentations of each side of the argument and to uncover the facts. He or she then suggests that a mediator or a conflict specialist come to the congregation to work out a compromise. Congregations rarely accept this advice. When they do, the mediator spends the first several sessions undoing the harm done because the congregation expected the judicatory leader simply to present a "winner take all" solution.

The higher-arbitration tool depends upon the availability of a judge who has the appropriate jurisdiction (both sides must obey) and who is willing to break his or her relationship with either of the parties as he or she renders a verdict. We see this kind of judge portrayed in courtroom dramas on television. Those of us who are parents, schoolteachers, or supervisors know that arbitrating is a necessary part of the job. The prevalence of higher arbitration in our culture makes it hard for both laity and clergy to understand how rarely it is helpful in the church. How often is a denominational official willing to jeopardize a relationship with a pastor or a congregation in order to proclaim the right verdict? It is also unusual for a pastor or other church leader to have both the jurisdiction and the necessary relational distancing to decide a case between two parishioners.

Unfortunately, people often call upon pastors and other church leaders to arbitrate minor conflicts. They come to us saying, "You know how Pete always does such and such and it bothers everybody because most people would prefer _____. Could you talk to him?" Notice that the language is that of mediation. Instead of asking a leader to judge or arbitrate, the person asks one to talk to Pete. Church leaders need to evaluate such requests very carefully. If I someone asks me to do this because I am the chairperson of a committee and the request relates to the committee, then he or she will likely expect me to deliver a judgment and arbitrate from on high. If the person insists that he or she wants to explore a compromise, then he or she should be willing to meet with the other person and with me and engage in mediation rather than arbitration (see below). Before agreeing to arbitrate, church leaders need to ask themselves the following questions:

1) **Is it clear to me and to all the parties involved that I have jurisdiction in this case?** Some people are professional arbitrators. They have a contract signed by both parties that states their authority before they proceed. Unless the church leader clearly spells out his or her authority, jurisdiction will become a problem.

2) **Am I willing to say to either party, "You are wrong," and experience the fallout of that statement on my relationship with the person or group?** Since arbitration is a legal process, it is incapable of making a decision without declaring that one party is wrong (or guilty) and the other party is right (or vindicated). Because arbitration decides an issue by only looking at the facts and ignores the relational component of conflict, it always leaves the parties feeling as if they personally either won or lost.

3) **Is it possible that a more fruitful and creative outcome may emerge if the leader uses another tool?** Arbitration is appropriate for those issues where speed and clarity are essential. Parents use their role as arbitrators to keep their children safe and to delineate clear boundaries in family matters. As they arbitrate between siblings, they nurture an understanding of personal space and property ownership in each child. In a similar fashion, pastors may need to arbitrate between committees and establish rules of confidentiality in order to protect administrative order in the church. Arbitration also is necessary in employment issues where the church needs to move quickly to a more effective staff arrangement.

One of the hidden assumptions of this tool, as well as the others in this section, is that matters of fact are at the core of the issue. If only we were able to see all the data or peer into the future, then we would know who was right and who was wrong. Arbitration is the most task-oriented and rational of all the conflict-resolution tools and therefore is the most contrary to any consideration of systemic and relational issues. The goal of arbitration is to decide who is right and to give them the toy. It considers irrelevant any history that does not immediately affect the decision. Yet, consideration of the past and of the story of how believers relate to each other and to the hopes and values of God's people is the very substance of church life. If conflict is to have any meaningful outcome for a congregation, then leaders must mine it for new insights about how to strengthen the love of the fellowship and further the mission that Christ left to his disciples.

Higher arbitration is a tool; it is only one tool of many. It is the foundation of our legal process and has a designated place in church law, especially when there has been an accusation of clergy misconduct. The role of arbitrator, however, excludes the peacemaking functions that are at the heart of the other tools for resolving conflict. As I have tried to explain in the first chapter, most congregational tensions originate in anxiety and transitional issues. When a pastor or interim minister tries to lead a congregation back to health, one of the first tasks is to talk people away from this legalistic approach to resolving their problems.

DEMOCRATIC PROCESS

I visited a progressive preschool recently and was surprised to see on the chalkboard the results of a vote they had taken as to whether snack time or recess would come next in their day. Recess had won fourteen to nine. I asked the teacher about the vote, and she told me that they were intentionally teaching the children the democratic process as a way of resolving their conflicts. Instead of teaching that the opinion of an authority (the teacher or an arbitrator) is the only one that matters, they gave the children opportunity to experiment with democracy and to learn its virtues and flaws. Even at this early age, children notice that participation in a collective process feels better than an authority figure telling them what to do. Each child watched the votes being tallied on the board and observed as the teacher assigned his or her opinion a value equal to the opinions of the other children. It is likely that many of these three to five-year-olds had no other occasion to experience equal participation in a collective process. Even when people find that they have lost their choice in an election, they still feel valued because their opinions were counted. The exercise also demonstrated to the children that to be in a community, whether a classroom or a congregation, is to surround oneself with others who legitimately see things differently. Church leaders who rely on hierarchical authority rather than democratic process need to be aware of the personal impact of this decision-making style on people. Advocating the pastor to act with greater authority or expecting a bishop to "bish" may not lead to a more efficient organization. People who have been excluded from the decision-making process are often reluctant to participate in implementation of the decision.

The democratic process, like arbitration, is adversarial in nature. It produces winners and losers. It has the potential of polarizing people into camps that remain long after the vote. Just deciding to settle an issue by a vote or a survey squelches the flow of ideas. Dialogue becomes subverted to the task of winning votes, and the group loses some of its natural ability to explore creative compromises or alternative actions. Task-oriented leaders and congregational cultures often rush things to a vote. However, a wiser course of action may be to appoint a study committee or to table the proposal until the group is closer to a consensus. From time to time, a church council will vote to approve something without considering how to implement it. They have forgotten that their purpose is to "council," that is, to engage in deliberation as an assembled body. They obviously thought they were meeting in order to vote and act. Sometimes the most liberating words the chairperson can say are these: "We don't have to decide this matter tonight. Let's set it aside and return to it when we can give it the discussion time it deserves."

The establishment of a timely democratic process, then, is not a cure-all for a conflicted church. Some congregations will find that establishing a predictable and trusted process for taking votes about controversial issues will be a step in the right direction. Democracy works best when it balances its relational and task-oriented sides. When we participate in a democratic process, we base some of our votes on the relationship we have with the person or group that is being elected or who puts forward a piece of legislation. The confidence or trust we place in certain individuals and the role that they have within the system are usually the major considerations for relationally-oriented congregations. Task-oriented congregations put a greater stock on the substance of the legislation or the stance that individuals being elected are likely to take when they face particular issues. As the level of conflict or anxiety rises in a task-oriented culture, people feel more compelled to ignore the relational or character component of their decisions. They act in accord with Sergeant Joe Friday of Dragnet who notably said, "Just the facts, ma'am." This approach subverts the larger processes needed in community. A pastor who wants to push forward a building project may stack the trustee board with individuals who will eventually vote for this adventure. What one plants, one eventually harvests. The church puts on the new addition but then struggles because the property trustees now have the wrong mixture of skills and personalities to maintain the whole facility properly. A more subtle problem for the task-oriented congregation is that once democracy

is stripped of its relational component, church life begins to feel imper-
sonal and eventually boring.

The highly relational congregation (chapter three) has an opposite
problem. Who is in favor of what, and how they relate to this or that
pillar of the church, concerns this congregation. Even when they take a
vote to put a new person in office or to act in some bold way, their use
of the countering actions of the matriarch or patriarch negate the democratic tool. They may vote to do a particular task, but unless they
involve the right personalities, they will not implement it.

Since the United Methodist Church, as well as most other American
Protestant church denominations, had their organizational birth in the
enlightenment culture of the late 1700s, its normal operating procedure
is democratic. Committees, annual conferences, and denominational
gatherings follow parliamentary procedure (Robert's Rules of Order)
and vote on issues. To a varying degree, all mainline denominations mix
the democratic process with the older tradition of valuing hierarchy and
using higher arbitration to make certain critical decisions. The two ways
of making decisions are always in opposition, and many of us in the
church value that tension, hoping to see this cultural tension preserved.
When we use a hierarchical process, such as in the making of appoint-
ments (the bishop and cabinet send clergy to congregations without the
congregation taking a vote), we depend on the spiritual integrity of
those in higher office to view things from a larger perspective. Trust
remains a core value in this relationship.

When the church uses a broad democratic process to decide major
issues, the results are often more global in perspective and more centrist
than they would seem. The downside of democratic or consensus-ori-
ented tools is that they allow interested parties to drag the process out
and may result in fuzzy policies and rules that no one can enforce. The
capacity of democracy to lengthen and deepen the discussion of issues
is a blessing, both in the local congregation and in the general church.
In spite of the homogenization of American culture brought about by
mass media, one can still observe at denominational gatherings a willingness to value diversity and note that those on the West Coast think

very differently from Appalachian easterners. Further, we all find ourselves forced by our democratic process to respect the globalization of
the church and the radically different perspectives of those who attend
our international gatherings from Africa, Asia, and Latin America.

What Democracy Requires

Like higher arbitration, democracy has certain prerequisites. James
Surowiecki, in his book *The Wisdom of Crowds* (Random House, 2004),
argues persuasively that when groups of people act collectively in making decisions, their chances of being right are far greater than when a few
experts decide for the group. His research also points to the importance
of the following:

- The voting group must be diverse. This means that the people we place on the administrative committees of the church
  should represent the various segments of the congregation's
  demographic. I think, for example, that it is more important
  that the people who make up the finance committee represent
  a variety of age and life backgrounds than that they all be
  financially astute. *The United Methodist Book of Discipline* recognizes the need for age and gender diversity on a number of
  committees. I would go a step further and attempt to salt the
  key committees of the church with people who are newcomers to the congregation. And a special word for congregations
  that have merged with other churches: Even after several
  decades, merged congregations do well to balance their committees to reflect all of the traditions present in the merged
  entity.

- Voters must not be unduly influenced by each other or by outsiders. Democracy collapses in the task-oriented church when
  a few "experts" influence the thinking of all others. Congregations often fall into "group think" were they fail to consider
  unpopular perspectives. As stated earlier, the relationally-
  oriented church falls apart when the reigning patriarch or

matriarch prevents the expression of diverse opinions. One also needs awareness that if the pastor is widely accepted as an outside expert or as someone with all the answers, this belief will reduce the power of the collective mind.

DISCERNMENT

In terms of a group process, spiritual discernment is a subset of the democratic process tools. Discernment is rooted in a theological concept that the Holy Spirit both resides in the individual and is incorporated into the collective mind or experience of the group. Discernment is not a tool that comes naturally to many groups today; people need to learn it. The leader of any committee or small group seeking to utilize spiritual discernment must begin by asking people to lay aside their natural competitive or individualistic approaches to the democratic process. The prayer of the participants is that the group's collective awareness of the will of God will be more valid than any individual's will. A key question that one may ask to guide the discernment process is, "In light of what God is doing, what are we to do?" Danny Morris and Chuck Olsen offer one discernment process in *"Discerning God's Will Together: A Spiritual Practice for the Church"* (Alban Institute: 1998). Their process calls for Bible reading, a clear statement of the issue, group prayer, conversation (or Christian conferencing), and silent prayer in a sequence prior to a response to the question of whether the group is ready to vote on the issue.

THE CONTINUUM TOOL

A less common, but often enlightening tool, invites people to stand on a line and physically demonstrate how strongly they hold their opinion about a proposition. For example, support for a proposal involving initiating a preschool program may divide the church. Rather than simply voting the idea up or down, people place themselves on a continuum. Those strongly convinced that the church should enter into this venture stand towards the right of the line. Those equally opposed move to the left. The area in the middle gives individuals the opportunity to express the mixture of feelings they hold regarding the preschool. The leader then alternates between the two ends of the line asking people to share why they chose to stand in that particular spot on the continuum.

This tool allows centrists to express their opinions. If the room feels lopsided against the idea, those who are proposing the preschool have the opportunity to hear the nature of the fears the concept is raising. Since the idea wasn't simply voted down, supporters now have the opportunity to pull the issue from decision-making and to revise the proposal to address the group concerns. Sometimes people may shift positions as they hear from others who have come to a different place on the issue. If the proposal succeeds, the opposition now has at least heard some of the more moderate participants express how they balanced their anxieties and their hopes on the issue.

One caution in using this tool: The continuum must be set up so that the two poles represent only the extreme position, that is, for those individuals who have no doubts whatsoever. The leader should encourage people to admit to being of two minds on difficult issues. If people simply move to extreme ends of the continuum, the group will become even more polarized than before the initiation of the process.

Fair Mediation

Mediation is another tool for resolving conflict that uses an impartial outside observer to facilitate discussion. Unlike an arbitrator, the person asked to mediate a substantial conflict arrives without any positional authority. His or her role is not to issue a judgment but to ensure that each side understands fully the concerns and aspirations of the other side. Mediators do not need to have any expertise in the subject of the conflict, nor is their personal faith or denomination usually an issue. They instead need to be trained mediators, and both sides of the issue need to perceive them as neutral. I would advise church leaders, after they have received permission from their own denominational office, to inquire about mediators who are ecumenically trained or available from secular consulting groups. Such a step assures a balanced neutrality that may not be possible from judicatory officials.

Often, the mediator's first tool is a process called "checking in." First, a person from one side presents one component of their own position without interruption. The other party listens and then restates what they have heard in their own words. The first party then confirms if the second party succeeded in understanding and restating what was said. If not, the first party restates their position until the second party successfully demonstrates their capability to understand what has been said. Next, the second party states one component of their position, and the first party "checks in" with them by restating that component. Each party takes turns presenting items without interruption and checks for understanding after making each point. Often, the adversaries are amazed by how much they share in common concerning the issues.

The mediator also works with the two parties to develop a list of shared values or interests. This list becomes the starting point to develop actions that both sides can support. For example, a church may be conflicted over whether they should retain or fire the current youth leader. During mediation, the opposing sides may discover that they share a concern for the safety of the youth. This common concern may lead to the establishment of policies that address this concern, regardless of whether this particular youth leader keeps the position.

Mediation is also a common tool for resolving the interpersonal conflicts that arise in relationship-oriented cultures. Here, the focus of the mediation is to help the warring parties understand the motivations and fears of their opponents. The exercise gives people the opportunity to speak about how certain events affect them. The mediator's facilitation creates a space where participants can understand past hurts and offer forgiveness. Mediation also has an educational role in helping relational cultures understand the family system behind their collective behavior.

Getting Values and Behavioral Expectations into Writing

Saying that the task-oriented culture has conflicts over issues of substance does not mean that their fights are less messy or lack the potential to deteriorate to mud-slinging contests. In even the most task-oriented of groups, there may be people with a low degree of emotional intelligence or those who believe so much in their visions that they manipulate others. Many secular corporations and non-profits operate within a competitive culture in which the ends justify the means, even when those means involve launching personal attacks on opponents. Those who have been rewarded for ill behavior elsewhere sometimes have a hard time adjusting to the nature of leadership that Christ gave to the church, a leadership that demonstrates the fruits of the Spirit.

Since task-oriented cultures focus on doing rather than being, they often fail to see the importance of shared values as the foundation for action. Part of a leader's task will be setting aside time, perhaps at a yearly planning retreat, to list the essential values of the congregation. Here are some questions to ask in such a discussion:

- What things go without saying as we conduct our business?

- Can you list five things that should always be true for this church?

- What is our highest priority?

One church stated that their highest value was, "Accepting people where they are and helping them to discover Christ." Each objective that they developed during their planning retreats needed to relate directly to this value. Throughout the year, as they began each church council meeting, they reviewed their priorities and the key values they had adopted. They began to appreciate the importance of the congregation's loving relationships as the foundation for their actions. This was a major perspective change.

The behaviors that the congregation permits in its political life flow directly out of its values. If its highest value is exhibiting the love of Christ, then behavior that is manipulative or denigrating of others is unacceptable. People who have a "dog eat dog" mindset may need to see a specific list of the behaviors this church finds unacceptable. It is a common practice to have youth in a fellowship or at camp develop a list of behaviors that will be unacceptable during the group's time together. This list often includes items such as "no put-downs" and "sharing equally any snacks." Unfortunately, many people entering into adulthood seem to have forgotten learned civil behavior. Working through such a behavioral covenant with the church council (or whatever group is having problems) can lead to dramatic improvement and a greater sense of the mission of the church.

Changing the Culture

Task-oriented cultures often attract people into leadership who value success over significance and winning over fair play. I once observed a friendly basketball game involving many of the leading men from a very task-oriented church. The use of elbows and street rules drew blood in every quarter. I later noticed some of the same individuals performing their church tasks with a similar competitive ferocity. As strange as it may sound, many people arrive in church office never having learned how to lose gracefully. This attitude not only makes a way for conflict within the church, but it also promotes polarized or "black-or-white" thinking.

The weakness of the task-oriented culture is its tendency to lower the value of individuals. It measures the components of the congregation objectively, weighing their contributions towards whatever goal the organization has. This goal may be financial, political, or theological. Some task-oriented congregations subject new members and new pastors to a litmus test of political opinions or theological beliefs. If the victim of this inquisition appears willing to help move the church in the desired direction (either to the left or to the right), then the leaders invite that person to join the club. If not, the task-oriented leadership organizes itself to render the new person ineffective.

In other task-oriented churches, the opinion of an individual only matters if he or she holds an office or is the deciding vote at a meeting. The task-oriented trustees, when they see those with handicapping conditions being barred entrance because of a staircase, ask, "I wonder what those people contribute towards the church. Is it cost-effective to put in a ramp if so little of our operating budget comes from people with disabilities?" This example of wrong-headed thinking may seem an extreme characterization, but task-oriented cultures permit their members to think this way, even if they don't include such statements in their minutes. Healthy congregations exert a continuous, negative social pressure on leaders who think of their members as mere objects. Healthy congregations are reluctant to appoint to church office someone who does not hold the congregation's values of diversity, justice, transparency, compassion, grace, and love toward all.

The key to shifting an overly task-oriented culture is to expose its competitive and destructive core. Jesus did this when he confronted the competitiveness of James and John:

> But Jesus called them to him and said, "You know that the rulers of the Gentiles lord it over them. It will not be so among you; but whoever wishes to be great among you must be your servant, and whoever wishes to be first among you must be your slave; just as the Son of Man came not to be served but to serve, and to give his life a ransom for many" (Matthew 20:25-28).

Leaders can utilize each tool provided in this chapter in ways that emphasize the value of fair play and loving relationships in the church. The church leader who is aware of this approach keeps encouraging people to look beyond resolving the current crisis issue and towards a form of behavior that is Christ-like. Leaders need to remind people constantly that the church does not mold itself after the world, and that what is successful in the eyes of the action-obsessed may be counter-productive to the work of the kingdom of God.

Test for the Task-Oriented Culture

Congregations do not live their whole lives in any one quadrant, nor is this system of placing a group's interactive dynamics onto a continuum between relationship and task-orientation meant to pigeonhole every decision-making body. We simply know that when people are passing through a task-oriented phase, the most frequent question is a variation of the children's travel question, "Are we there yet?"

Task-oriented people and relational-oriented people ride together in the same vehicle (the church). They take turns as to who dominates the conversation. While the emotionally mature may value both the beauty of the ride and the prospect of getting somewhere, the kids in the backseat can make things miserable by focusing the congregation's entire attention on achieving certain objectives. I am hopeful that this perspective will be valuable to you in resolving the conflicts that arise in this quadrant.

CHAPTER THREE

Quadrant Two: Fighting Like Family and the Culture of Cliques

Good fences make good neighbors.

Robert Frost ("Mending Wall")

The Bells of Saint U

Saint U is the smallest church on a four-point charge, and the most distant from the parsonage. The day the new pastor arrived in town she received a phone call from Ed, who said, "You know those bells you got are too loud." Pastor Joy tried to imagine how she had suddenly become the owner of noisy bells. Ed continued, "You have to realize that my wife is an invalid, and they have them set to go off first thing in the morning, noon, and night, and we can't take it much more. You do something about it, pastor. Goodbye." The next Sunday, Joy discovered that St. U did indeed have a carillon. It sat at the rear of the one-room church in a handsome metal box. It had wires running up to a belfry where, Pastor Joy assumed, speakers broadcast the pealing renditions of the hymns to the faithful. Through the locked glass front, she could see a clock face with a mechanism for setting the time of the chimes and their volume. She noted that the volume knob was in the dead-center position. Later that day, she had a long visit with Ed and his wife. It was a pleasant time as Ed regaled the new pastor with stories about various people in the church, half of whom were his relatives. It ended with Joy determined to resolve the issue at the next church council and Ed saying how much they enjoyed visits from the pastor.

The council meeting became tense when Joy said she had a small issue to bring up that involved the neighborliness of the church. John argued that money from his mother's memorial fund had purchased the carillon for the expressed purpose of comforting the residents of the local nursing home. John's mother had spent her final years at this facility, located half a mile across the valley. John said, "You should go and visit those people. They'll tell how much they appreciate our chimes." In the end, the council gave the pastor permission to experiment with the volume control to see if she couldn't find a happy medium. John later pulled the pastor aside and in a confidential whisper said, "The real problem is that Ed is an atheist. He doesn't like us playing hymns on our chimes."

Over the next four years, the volume control moved up and down. Joy spent hours listening to the chimes from different locations and under various atmospheric conditions. On two occasions the carillon's locked door was forcibly sprung and the volume changed. For months on end, John's rather large family would boycott church in protest over the pastor and the chimes. Joy became more and more enmeshed in what she discovered was a family feud. She felt as if she were peeling an onion as she learned who was related to whom and how the animosity between John and Ed was based on a rivalry that extended back several generations. Joy eventually moved on, leaving the volume knob set at dead center.

Reckoning with the System

All churches are family systems. Even when people are not related and have little personal contact beyond the activities of a congregation, their relational history still heavily influences them. Past slights or favors require future payback, and who groups together with whom can govern even the most objective nuts-and-bolts decisions of a church. Family ties, age, ethnicity, where people work, and where people live can subdivide congregations into voting blocks. The wise church leader is willing to see these groupings for what they are: relational networks. A congregation cannot have a strong sense of community without fostering some relational cliques. They are to community life what fire has been to human civilization: a great force for good or evil. Ever since fire's discovery, humanity has developed building codes and better technology to contain this gift. Still, homes and forests burn down, and people use fire for both good and evil.

Relational networks become evil when they:

- Become exclusive cliques, valuing their membership above other people in the congregation;

- Foster a patronizing attitude, particularly when church staff are seen as dependents to be cared for rather than as employees to be compensated for their work;

- Use inappropriate means to manipulate church decisions;

- Are racist, sexist, or actively engaged in the denigration of others;

- Refuse to be transparent about their values and what they hope to achieve;

- Perpetuate their control by isolating the church from its community context and denominational body.

This list certainly does not encompass all the ways relational groupings exceed their beneficial roles and become problematic. Rather than categorizing various forms of dysfunction, let me state that all special relationships—that is cliques—have a potential to distract the church from its original task. If the church becomes a chapel, meeting the private needs of its dominant family, then it will fail to be in mission to redeem the world. If self-centered or unethical people are able to use their relational network to run the church, most of what the church does will serve them instead of the cause of Christ. If a congregation does not model Jesus' love for all people, then it cannot speak about his love at all. If the unstated goals of some in the church become the real business of the church, then the church will never be about the business of making disciples.

One telltale sign that a church has become too relationally oriented is in passive-aggressive behavior towards newcomers and outsiders (including the pastor). The lay-leadership committee may be quick to ask new members to serve on various committees, but anything important that needs to be done has to pass through the trustees or another long-term officer. Old-guard members hold these positions, and they use their personal influence to block whatever their clique does not support. Often task-oriented pastors complain that the continuous resistance of the ruling clan fritters away their best efforts to lead the church into the modern era. The culture of cliques rarely goes to war to block progress, but it can slow it down to a snail's pace. It rigs the system to make certain groups or key people happy, rather than to achieve results.

This is not exclusively a small-membership church problem. Even though small-membership churches as a group are more relationship-oriented than larger congregations, they can embody a healthy openness to outsiders and a joy for achieving missional tasks. I have come to believe that when a church has an average worship attendance of less than seventy-five, its normal balance point between task-orientation and relationship-orientation shifts in the direction of relationships. In other words, a small-membership church can be effective at making disciples, even though its culture will appear to be excessively relationship-oriented to an outside observer. I once served as pastor of a small-membership church where half the people were related to one extended family, and many of the church activities felt like extensions of that family's gatherings. However, they ran the church meetings well and encouraged free discussion. They regularly achieved goals that the matriarch of the family did not support and had no difficulty assimilating new members.

The evils listed above, however, are always destructive, no matter what the size of the congregation. They set the stage for destructive conflict even when all parties seem calm and reasonable. In society, it is helpful to view intractable problems such as racism as both the fault of sinful people and the fault of self-perpetuating systems. In the church, it is important not to be so hung up on the immaturity of the key players that we fail to see the system that allows them to behave as they do.

Shifting the task versus relationship-orientation balancing point of a congregation back to a point where the church can function is a systemic problem. Instead of immediately denouncing the manipulative behavior of the reigning patriarch, a church leader does well to step back and observe the congregation as a whole. Newcomers to a longstanding feud often assume they can develop a compromise or decide problematic issues on a case-by-case basis. The rational new pastor hopes to appear fair-minded by siding first with one side and then with the other. The time that Pastor Joy spent measuring the decibels of the chimes of St. U and adjusting the volume knob may have been better spent peeling the onion of the congregation's history. Success for her would not occur in finding the perfect compromise setting but in leading the church council to develop better decision-making skills.

What Fuels Relational Conflict

Dante reserved a special place in hell for those who sow division within close-knit communities. In one of the most gruesome cantos of the *Inferno*, he tells how those condemned are continuously dismembered. A demon flays them with a sword and then makes them walk the full circle of hell, only to return to their starting place to flay them again. With this punishment, Dante reinforces the idea that conflict is often circular and repetitious. One realizes, with horror, that this is hell's most perfect punishment because those who divide families, congregations, and nations are dismembering the communal bodies that we as humans need to remain sane (see *Inferno*, Canto XXVIII). We humans are, by nature, social animals. Our deeper instinct to form fellowships counterbalances our need for independence and self-gratification. Those who cut the fabric of congregational relationships, however unintentionally, damage something of greater value to the church than its stained-glass windows, cathedral roof, or honored traditions.

When it is healthy, a congregation is both inviting to newcomers and respectful of the place occupied by long-term members. The healthy church intentionally provides portals for outsiders to enter into the fellowship. It also works to assimilate new people further into the work and committees of the church. The fabric of even the healthiest church, however, is not a seamless, undifferentiated whole. Each congregation has its patterns of relationships that the outsider has to learn. The outsider will eventually discover the long-running tensions between the various players in church leadership. In the healthy congregation, these family feuds never interrupt the assimilation of the newcomer. The church fulfills its role of making disciples, however slowly, by incorporating the newcomer into a fellowship family that nurtures faith.

In the relationally over-functioning congregation, the congregation's obsession with tribal allegiances sidetracks the natural disciple-making process. It coerces people to join one group or another. Members face rejection if they don't vote along family lines. In many small-membership churches, the relationships that long-time members have in their natural families spill over and dominate the body politic of the congregation. What is unhealthy in their homes, such as codependency, verbal abuse, and passive-aggressive behavior, is replicated on the larger stage of the church. Fights begun elsewhere continue at the potluck supper and in the church council meeting. In congregations of every size, there are individuals who, because they have little family outside the church (or an extremely dysfunctional home life), have decided to make the congregation their "real" family. This emotional transference can make them vulnerable to the manipulation of others. It can also lock them into rigid and unreasonable behavior as they try to force the pastor and staff to live up to their expectations.

Many pastors have noted how their churches mirror the television series "Survivor." They watch as different factions scheme to vote people off the island. The church fellowship splinters into alliances and tribal voting blocks. In working with a congregation that has become a culture of cliques, the trick is to shift the goal away from survival and toward disciple-making. At its worst, the relationally dysfunctional congregation becomes a closed fiefdom. Newcomers and pastors are mere spectators of the real show. The church tolerates them but never assimilates or respects them.

Relationally-oriented congregations often reduce their tasks down to one: survival. Where task-oriented people think of the church in terms of what it does, the residents of this quadrant speak of the church in terms of what it is. Their mission serves their tribal identity. They will say, "My family has belonged to this church for ten generations," or "We need to sing this hymn on Sunday because it is so-and-so's favorite." Keeping the doors open and the right clan in control occupies them full-time. The key leaders would rather see the church become ineffectual than see it change to the point where their clique does not feel appreciated. To this end, they will vote people off the island, even if those people are faithful and highly talented.

When conflict erupts, the immediate goal may be to open dialogue and negotiate a reduction of hostilities between the cliques. Leaders need to squelch any behavior that votes people off the island. The long-range goal is to reestablish the disciple-making tasks of the church. It is neither wise nor reasonable to expect people to stop valuing their family cliques, but it is possible to shift this loving energy towards the task of assimilating new members. This suggests a three-step process for healing relationally-oriented conflicts:

1) Seek to understand the family system and identify the key issues that each group is striving to control. When we see manipulative or irrational behavior, there is often some unmet root need. This root issue usually relates in some way to security. The family that seeks to control church finances, for example, may have issues relating to how mismanagement has caused a loss in the home, workplace, or church in the past. Getting these fears into open conversation so that all parties recognize what has been hidden is the first step

towards healing. People begin to share freely emotional baggage and irrational fears. As mentioned in chapter one, church leaders need to listen non-defensively to this flow of fear. This step moves the whole church toward health and wholeness, the shalom promised by Jesus.

2) Gradually shift the focus of church dialogue from survival toward mission. Weekly worship should have an outward orientation. Instead of allowing people to view the church as a sanctuary that shelters them from a scary world, the messages and the liturgy should propel people in the direction of caring for their neighbors. Leaders should address and set aside fears that the church may close. The relationally-oriented church should channel its energy and resources toward the needs of people who may never become a part of one of their cliques.

3) Develop new procedures and decision-making processes that include outsiders and respect the concerns of long-term members. I often push the nominations committee to add at least one newcomer (less than two years in the congregation) to each of the key committees of the church. The difficulty they have in fulfilling this task often leads to healthy discussion about how the church assimilates new members. Most communities have a certain transient population, such as people who regularly vacation near the church, college students, or military families. What has your congregation done intentionally to include these people into its life? Pairing long-term members with transient individuals may provide both a great outreach and an attitudinal adjustment to the ingrown congregation.

The Terrors of Triangulation

Relational cultures love to wrap up their pastors and church staff in a game called "triangulation." This is where person A asks the pastor or other church leader to mediate a dispute that they are having with person B. The mediating church leader becomes the "monkey in the middle." It is their duty to go to person B and jeopardize their own relationship with B in order to make A happy. No sensible person would agree to be the monkey if it weren't for the skill that quadrant-three dwellers have in camouflaging the game. They say:

- My husband B loves your sermons, Pastor. If you were to ask him to stop smoking, I think he would finally quit.

- B and I are no longer speaking, and I want to make peace with her. Will you go to her for me and say . . . ?

- My son is in the youth group, and for some reason he doesn't want to be in the school band this year. Could you talk to him and find out if there is some problem?

- The organist is getting too old for the job. We don't want to fire her outright. It's your job, Pastor, to talk to her and cushion the blow. Maybe if you were to speak to her, she would resign on her own.

Church leaders need to be vigilant against triangulation, not only because they may lack the necessary mediation skills, but also because in achieving the stated objective they may cause unforeseen relational rifts. The same people who sent the pastor on the mission to talk with the organist will also be the ones who tar and feather him. The story will circulate about how the pastor cruelly broke that faithful saint's heart. In mediating with the youth who has dropped out of band, the youth leader will be acting like a parental spy and violating rules of confidentiality. Every game of triangulation has its loser, and it is rarely A or B.

Triangulation also stunts the development of A and B's relational skills. As long as they have a monkey in the middle, they don't have to learn how to communicate. People trained in mediation use their skills to facilitate direct communication between parties. As we shall see later, Jesus specifically outlines tools for reconciliation that avoid triangulation (see Matthew 18:15-20). The goal is to train people to communicate directly with the person with whom they disagree.

Boundary Crossers

Highly-relational cultures often expect their leaders to live without boundaries. Consider the relationship Pastor Joy inherited with Esther, the oldest member of St. U. Esther was not a member of either side of the carillon controversy at St. U, but she did like to call Pastor Joy every Friday morning to report on the week's skirmishes. Fridays were the pastor's day off. Esther knew how to package her call so that it circumvented Joy's expressed instructions only to be bothered if there were an emergency. She was also an expert at crossing the border and intruding into the personal affairs of Joy's family.

Esther's continuous incursions were another example of the insider versus outsider game that relationally-oriented congregations play with those who are new to the system. Those who grew up in the community have already established the borders they have with each other. They have high fences that guard their personal lives against intruders from opposing cliques. With the members of their own clique, however, they have an openbackdoor policy, accepting even the most intrusive behavior. A relational culture defines a "gossip" as someone who takes secrets and tells them to a member of another clique. This is why these congregations often invite pastors to preach sermons against gossip.

When outsiders enter the community, they become fair game for border incursions. Since they do not belong to your clique, you can share personal information about them without being a gossip. Information is power. You can use it to adopt outsiders temporarily into your clique. You can also use it to blackmail outsiders and control their behavior. If you can share embarrassing or confidential information about the new pastor, then you can diminish his or her authority or potential to disrupt the current status quo. Often, however, the motivation for such behavior is simply loneliness or curiosity.

Many pastors find themselves vulnerable to this manipulation because they want their congregations to like and accept them. It is better for new pastors initially to form stiff boundaries, which they can loosen when they know the system. Conflict is a frequent visitor to the relational culture. If one of the church's cliques adopts a pastor he or she failed to maintain self-differentiation; then the pastor is no longer available to act constructively to heal any issue. Further, many pastors find themselves blindsided when they discover how much their family members resent the way that church members have intruded into their personal space and time.

Dysfunctional People

In general, relational cultures have a high tolerance for individuals who act inappropriately. Within tight-knit societies, familiarity does not breed contempt. Rather, it fosters expressions of what the culture considers normal. They may say about an abusive person, "Well, he's always had a short temper, but we know how to handle him." Or they may justify their failure to remove a manipulative church leader, saying, "She does so much around here. We couldn't get along without her." There is a certain counterintuitive logic in these statements. Every person plays a role within the system. The leaders know that in closed systems, someone has to occupy the role of the troublemaker and the role of the hero.

Pastors and other leaders who arrive from outside the system need to be cautious. Others will view any attempt to fix or ostracize the troublesome individual as an attack on the entire congregational network. The long-term goal is to get the congregation to realize that they have become a closed system. Dysfunctional people frighten newcomers away, both diminishing and isolating the church. The lay leadership's failure to contain the inappropriate behavior of this member hurts the very community the congregation wants to preserve. Leaders must understand that those who behave badly rarely have an interest in seeing the church grow. They will time their outbursts to scare new people away. It takes courage to confront them about the lasting effect they are having on the church's mission.

In the meantime, relationship-oriented congregations need empowerment to develop behavioral covenants (see chapter two). They can agree together that certain behaviors are inappropriate and create a covenant that applies to everyone, including the dysfunctional individual. In dealing with difficult people, the pastor or other church staff must be extremely cautious not to be caught in a triangulated relationship. People are always quick to ask those with some authority to step in and rescue or fix situations. Wise leaders avoid this trap and patiently teach the appropriate board or committee to present a unified front in dealing with the offender.

Test for a Relational Culture

The people in small-membership churches tend to value relationships above tasks. They will make statements such as "We're just one happy family here," or "The reason we come here rather than the big church is because we like knowing everybody." This attitude is normal in churches with up to seventy-five in attendance, and it is a God-sent blessing for larger congregations. In detail, I have described the pathology of Christian groups that focus on the needs of manipulative people and the family clan to the exclusion of the church's mission. This loss of the high calling can be fatal, and wise leaders should address it, even if the church is not currently in conflict.

In general, you will know that you are in this quadrant when people fail to ask questions about whether a course of action will be effective or fruitful for the church. If the quest to make the matriarch or themselves feel good about things describes the mood of the group, then it is stuck in the relational culture. Churches need to have goals. They cannot simply settle down and enjoy their own company. When a congregation seeks to preserve this self-satisfied state, it inevitably drifts left into quadrant two, the place of apathy. As I will explain in the next chapter, this is where conflict becomes most absurd and where the church is in the greatest danger.

CHAPTER FOUR

Quadrant Three: The culture of Apathy

Things fall apart; the center cannot hold;
. . . The best lack all conviction, while the worst
Are full of passionate intensity.

William Butler Yeats ("The Second Coming")

Apathy is not a normal condition for a congregation. Quadrant two is inherently a state of disease and disruption. The gospel of Jesus Christ is a thing of excitement. It requires our best. The joy of Christian fellowship and the challenge of making new disciples give a sense of purpose to healthy congregations. Yet many churches appear dull and burned out. They are content to do the minimum for mission, accept the most lackluster of pastoral leaders, and receive no new members by profession of faith year after year. When they actually do become excited, what motivates them is the fear that they may close. This fear of death, coupled with the dull ache of boredom, drives them to have silly conflicts. They fall victim to explosive episodes and grand delusions. They may tilt at windmills or engage in ritual cannibalism. To paraphrase Yeats, "things fall apart," and congregational arguments are full of "passionate intensity."

This condition of congregational apathy has several causes. Long-term, ineffective pastoral leadership gradually leads some churches into lower expectations. They may have a pastor who is extremely likable but not challenging. The body as a whole drifts towards retirement. Often, the laity is aware of the challenges the next pastor will face in replacing the beloved Rev. Meekly Peaceful. Rarely do they receive guidance by their denominational officials into how to have a productive transition. (I wrote about this in *The Church Transition Workbook*.) They will likely per-ceive the next pastor as youthful, task-oriented, and unrealistic, even though he or she may be relatively the same age and of the same tem-perament as his or her predecessor.

Other churches have seemingly the opposite problem. A pastor or series of pastors leads them to take on more than their appropriate duties. These leaders may be openly autocratic and micro-manage all of the church's business. More often, they are simply codependent and prone to over-function. (*Peter's Boat*, another book in this series, focuses on this matter.) Over-functioning clergy stymie what church members expect of their collective efforts. Even the smallest congre-gation deserves to do more than that which the pastor can do alone. This type of situation usually remains peaceful until the problem-pastor leaves. The new reality of more appropriate clergy leadership creates conflict as people cry out, "We never had to do these things before."

The more frequent cause of apathy in the church is unhealed trauma. Traumas come in various forms, but their lasting effect is to cre-ate a congregational culture that is risk-averse and unwilling to commit to both relational ties and missional tasks.

- A previous pastor may have been caught in some type of mis-conduct and then quickly replaced. The next pastor is then expected to sweep the matter quickly under the carpet. Secrets are not healthy for the development of family sys-tems, whether a nuclear or church family. The congregation does not have a chance to express appropriately its anger or grief. This situation instills within the culture a distrust of denominational and pastoral leadership. Their unexpressed grief also pops up in silly quarrels over trivial issues.

• The traditional industry of a town may have closed, and the emerging new economy may be empowering people of a different culture than the church's membership. Many churches in this situation essentially shut down. They maintain a worship service and traditional style of ministry that fail to connect with their context. The anger that people feel about what is happening to the neighborhood doesn't have a forum where it can be talked about or given a theological perspective. Isolated within its stained-glass walls, the church becomes a hotbed of in-fighting and stupid conflicts.

• A congregation may have faced a critical decision when it could have taken a leap forward and instead chose to continue on the same old course. This may have been a decision to build or relocate to expand its ministries. Perhaps a merger proposal would have created a more viable, combined congregation. A fire or flood may have created the opportunity to take the insurance money and not simply replace the old, but instead make decisions that would serve the future. Opportunities rejected are the hidden traumas of a congregation's history. They leave a sour taste in the mouth, which continues for decades.

Spiritual Vacuum

Nature, it is said, abhors a vacuum. This means that a church, devoid of loving relationship or missional purpose, will find some kind of conflict to attract attention. Jesus puts this poignantly in a parable in Luke:

> "When the unclean spirit has gone out of a person, it wanders through waterless regions looking for a resting place, but not finding any, it says, 'I will return to my house from which I came.' When it comes, it finds it swept and put in order. Then it goes and brings seven

other spirits more evil than itself, and they enter and live
there; and the last state of that person is worse than the
first" (Luke 11:24-26).

The conflicts that occur in an apathetic church are interesting and
varied. They can feel like seven demons on a rampage. I cannot suggest
any one trick for resolving the immediate conflict. Instead, church leaders have to try one thing after another until they find a way to settle
people down. When there is a moment of peace, however, the wise
church leader sets people on the path of addressing the core issue, which
is the spiritual vacuum at the heart of the congregation.

Leaving Quadrant Two

Jesus' words suggest that the cure for an apathetic culture must be a
spiritual one. In my other books, I have written extensively about the theology of transition that is necessary to heal the residual grief residing in
the congregation. When a church is parked in this quadrant, members
need scriptural guidance to assess their purpose for existence. They need
to develop both a community of mutual trust and a sense of God-given
mission. This process suggests the following steps:

1) Do the congregation's history. Create an appropriate forum
   to talk about the trauma even if it happened years ago.
   Having dug up some dirt, plant some healing. Hold an event
   where people can celebrate their history and recognize what
   is good about their traditions and values. Create a church-his-
   tory timeline, collect old photographs, and have a dinner
   where people can share stories about how the church used to
   be.

2) Lead people toward greater spiritual passion. Restore expectation for prayer and a sense of the relevance of scripture.
   Teach people the importance of Christian witness and appropriate ways to reach out within their culture. (For more on
   spiritual passion, see *Ezekiel's Bones*, which is another book in
   the Congregational Leaders Empowered to Change series.)

3) Evaluate and develop functional organizational structures. Create a path to move people from the vision toward actual implementation. (My book, *Saul's Armor*, helps with this task.)

The Test for a Culture of Apathy

You know you have entered the culture of apathy when you hear frequents complaints about all that the people have to do. Many churches fail to recruit and train new leadership, and the burden of keeping the church going often falls to the faithful few. These people rarely complain or do so with good humor as long as they see real mission and fellowship because of their efforts. In the church of quadrant two, however, people complain even when the tasks are few and the labor is light. They ask, "Why do we have so many church meetings?" even though their attendance at those meetings is rare. They say, "The church is always asking for money," even though their personal stewardship is poor. Every church has some members and even a few leaders with an "I couldn't care less" attitude. What is dangerous is when this disease has completely infected the congregational culture. The church is meant to be faithful, effective, and fruitful. We often think that conflict is the thing that is keeping us from being that way, when it is merely a symptom of a system that has lost its purpose.

CHAPTER FIVE

Quadrant Four: Beyond the Happy Medium

Compromise makes a good umbrella, but a poor roof.

James Russell Lowell

It would be a terrible mistake to think that solving church conflict is simply a matter of finding a balance between relational orientation and the pursuit of missional tasks. Each of the cultural quadrants described has limited the productivity of the church and bred their own forms of disharmony. Shifting the culture has usually involved getting people to see the other side of the task-relationship orientation continuum. But no congregation lives in a state of perfect balance between relationship and task orientation. When a church resolves its current conflict or crisis, it moves toward a natural center where it feels at home. The home place cannot be a resting place. The faithful congregation engages in missional tasks and then discovers as it acts that its members love each other. The symbiosis between mission and relationship is the genius of Christ's church.

Jesus called his first disciples into a learning environment where they discovered both the importance of mission (making other disciples for the kingdom of God) and the joyful life of Christian fellowship. Jesus wanted his faithful twelve to love each other intensely, but he also asked them to split up and carry the gospel to the far corners of the earth. In the first few chapters of Acts, the early church is a relationally intense fellowship where ". . . those who believed were of one heart and soul . . ." (Acts 4:32 NRSV). After the martyrdom of Steven, the external conflict of persecution scatters the apostles. Each traveling evangelist has to reproduce a relational-oriented fellowship in the context of his mission field. As the newly-birthed congregation develops structure, it also learns how to be task-oriented and engage in its own mission work. Therefore, we see the Apostle Paul writing to the relationally-minded Corinthians, urging them to make a contribution towards the needs of the people in Jerusalem whom they have never met (2 Corinthians 8–9).

Clear Expectations

It is hard for pastors and programmatic church staff to lead the church toward quadrant four without clear role expectations. The key lay leadership must be on the same page as their pastor about the tasks they need to perform and the relationships they need to maintain. Pastor-parish relations committees rarely appreciate that helping people do well at their work involves continuously negotiating both the task-oriented and the relationship-oriented sides of their role. The pastor in his previous parish may have been responsible for relating to the youth group and had an extensive list of tasks related to the nurturing component of that congregation. He may be unaware that this work will be inappropriate in his new context. Besides stepping on the toes of the effective laypersons in those positions, he may be leaving tasks undone that are critical to the health of this new parish. Congregational life has become increasingly complex and diverse over the last forty years, and the role that was effective in one context will not work in another. For the first year after a new pastor or church staffperson arrives, there should be monthly check-in meetings with the pastoral-relations committee to discuss priorities and expectations. From time to time these discussions will add or subtract items from the written "job description" that the church maintains for each position. The lasting value of these meetings is the way they flesh out nebulous terms, such as "visiting the shut-ins" and "overseeing the outreach program."

Church employees often fail to meet expectations. This is seldom a matter of sheer laziness or incompetence. When a person does not know what others expect, he or she will tend to retreat to a place of safety. We see this in the pastor who devotes all of her time to the youth group or who only visits those in a retirement home. Each time an employee fails to meet someone's expectations, he or she gets a little "zap." This "zap" may be in the form of a note or an off-handed comment repeated through three other people before it makes its way back to the employee. If the employees have a regularly scheduled (monthly for the first year) role-clarity meeting with the staff-relations committee, then they can get a reality check on these "zaps." What comments are legitimate indicators of where work needs to be done differently or the role redefined? How can employees hone their skills to meet expectations?

This collaborative approach to the tasks and relationships of a position has the potential to squelch serious conflict. Usually, pastors and church staff take their "zaps" and store them away in the backroom of their psyches. When that dark place becomes full, they become anxious and reactive (see chapter one). They may lash out at the major source of criticism, but more often, they will redirect their anger toward an innocent party (bark at the secretary, snap at the spouse, kick the fire hydrant, and so forth). Some people have a passive-aggressive response to misunderstood or unrealistic role expectations; they will say or do whatever answers the immediate complaint but secretly sabotage any effort to meet that need.

When conflict emerges and the shared role expectations that support performance of a job utterly collapse, some people flee, and other people remain to fight a cold war. Church leaders who are of the silent and World War II generations tend to stay put and enter a standoff with their opponents. Those born after 1948 are more likely to take flight.

The fact that the average length of pastoral stay in the United Methodist church is under four years speaks volumes about one denomination's failure to provide mechanisms for negotiating clear role expectations.

Getting to Growth

Church leaders learn best how to maintain relational networks while achieving missional tasks when some form of covenant discipleship involves them. This means having the key leaders participate in a small group (less than twelve people) where members hold one another accountable for personal spiritual growth and give each other an opportunity to do some portion of the church's missional work as a team. A variation on covenant discipleship groups known as the *L3 Leadership Incubator* (Discipleship Resources, 2006) joins relational values and missional tasks. Over the course of eighteen months, participants form a task-oriented fellowship. Leaders exit the incubator experience knowing what it is like to be in a group that both loves and acts. This knowledge can transfer to every aspect of the church's life.

True quadrant-four churches replicate Jesus' work with his disciples. They insist that all of their key leaders participate in small groups. They farm out to teams much of their outreach work and nurturing tasks. The church intentionally works to foster a community environment at every level. Children find the church school to be a place where they dialogue around the table and participate in decision-making. The youth group goes on mission trips designed to be team experiences. Each of the adult programs has both a task and a relational component. The key to quadrant four is not avoiding conflict by compromise, but utilizing diversity and strong interpersonal relationships to form effective and fruitful ministries.

CHAPTER SIX

Divine Tools for Reconciliation

If you can keep your head when all about you are losing theirs and
blaming it on you . . . Yours is the earth and everything that's in it.

Rudyard Kipling ("If")

So when you are offering your gift at the altar, if you remember that
your brother or sister has something against you, leave your gift there
before the altar and go; first be reconciled to your brother or sister,
and then come and offer your gift.

Matthew 5:23-24

Jesus said a great deal about the nature of conflict, particularly
about how it interferes with the participant's personal relationship with
God. Much of what he said applies to the group dynamics that one
encounters during congregational conflict. What Jesus said supersedes
anything that I have written in this book. I am convinced that if church
leaders fully understood and applied the teachings of our Lord, conflicts
would be both our relational and our substantial channeled toward fruitful behavior. All of what Jesus says on this topic is relevant, much of it

is difficult, and none of it is dispensable.

Jesus' gospel on conflict contains three core concepts:

- **All of us have the ability to determine our own behavior.**
  Jesus always makes us responsible for our response to ill treatment. His teachings do not permit us to say, "I did this
  because they . . . " Jesus also undercuts the circular nature of
  revenge that fuels so many church fights. He says, "You have
  heard that it was said, 'An eye for eye and a tooth for tooth.'
  But I say to you . . . if anyone forces you to go one mile, go
  also the second mile" (Matthew 5:38, 41). Jesus insists that
  we treat others with kindness that disregards their treatment
  of us or their position in a controversy. He says flatly, "Do
  to others as you would have them do to you" (Luke 6:31).

- **We have the capacity to forgive anyone "from our heart."**
  Much has been written about Jesus' radical approach to forgiveness. He did not offer any loophole around the simple
  statement that we must always forgive completely. Jesus
  would not command it if he did not think we were capable
  of it.

- **We can initiate systemic change through radical loving
  behavior.** When Jesus teaches about turning the other cheek,
  he does it within the context of initiating a movement of
  people who will transform the world by their vision of the
  kingdom of God (Matthew 5—7). We can view the radical
  aspects of Jesus' ministry, such as his acceptance of known
  sinners and utilization of irreligious people, as deliberate
  actions to change a cruel social system. He literally shamed
  his opponents into adjusting their structures to be more loving. This concept was foundational for the civil disobedience
  practiced by Gandhi and Martin Luther King Jr. It also has
  profound implications for shifting the conflicted systems of
  a local church.

Apologies

Jesus never uses the word *apology*. Our normal process of reconciliation centers on the apology as its first step. We were taught as children that if we do something wrong, our first step is to apologize. We quickly surmised from this lesson that if someone wrongs us, our first step was to wait for an apology. Unfortunately, few of us receive any instruction as to what to do when it is not clear who ought to apologize or when miscommunication rather than malice is at the heart of the issue. Placing our focus upon this artificial construct called "the apology" locks us into an adversarial process each time a situation requires reconciliation. Because the person who apologizes has to be the primary offender, we find ourselves marshalling arguments as to who is the wrongdoer.

Jesus begins in a different place. He begins with the church, and specifically the altar, which symbolizes our relationship with God. If I am a person who has a relationship with God, then occasionally I will discover that a failure in the relationship that I have with someone else will interfere and preempt my ability to worship God. Jesus does not say, "First determine who caused this failure." Instead, he says, "First, go," which implies that we reconnect with that other person. We must first discover common ground for dialogue. Then we enter into reconciliation, which may involve listening to the other person tell of our wrongdoing. Then we may speak our own words of confession and reconciliation. The activity of reopening honest conversation takes precedence over any interest we may have in assigning blame.

In the church, we must learn to avoid any adversarial process that fixes blame. A process is adversarial if its outcome diminishes the respect due to those on the losing side or gives greater honor to those who win. Any legal process is by definition adversarial because it designates one side as wrong or guilty while the other is justified or acquitted. Life rarely has the purity of a chess game, where every piece gained by one side mirrors a loss for the other. Jesus talks about love in a way that excludes any adversarial approach to our relationships.

The game of waiting for someone to make an apology is adversarial. It expects someone else to do something that will make him or her the loser in the game. How can we avoid this competitive quality to our relationships when we are playing our role in response to someone's behavior? When we do something wrong to others, we need to go and communicate both our sorrow for their pain and our plan to change our behavior in the future (repentance). When others wrong us, we need to accept our own pain as our own experience. We may need to protect ourselves by adjusting our vulnerability to them and others like them in the future. At any rate, we need to avoid the temptation to comfort ourselves by thinking of them as evil or losers. If they offer an apology, our acceptance of that apology should involve helping them honor themselves (not seeing themselves as losers in the situation) and experience restoration in the eyes of others who may have heard of the conflict.

Jesus' Conflict-Resolution Tool

In Matthew 18:15-20, Jesus provides an alternative tool for conflict resolution in the church. We can organize this process into the following steps:

1) The person offended by someone should go to that person directly and avoid triangulation or general gossip. Individual dialogue should be the first step in resolving both substantial differences of opinion about church policy, as well as any relational problems that are disrupting the fellowship. Timely and direct discussions between two individuals who are in conflict should resolve most issues. Training church leaders to go directly to the person with whom they have a problem is a key step in building a civil congregational culture. Teach church leaders how to use "I" statements in such confrontations. Instead of telling the offender that their behavior bothered others, the church leader shares how he or she personally experienced the situation and owns his or her feelings.

2) If the first step fails to resolve the issue, the leader enlists one or two other trusted persons to come and witness a second meeting with the offender. On this occasion, the additional

persons are not there to overpower the offender, but to observe and facilitate the communication process. They may utilize the checking-in process described in the mediation section of chapter two. They also search for creative compromises and provide prayer support for the resolution of the issue.

3) Only when steps one and two have been faithfully followed is an offended person allowed to bring the situation to an official board or committee of the church. Sometimes church members will have a difficulty with the pastor. If they approach the pastoral-relations chairperson or the judicatory supervisor (district superintendent in the United Methodist Church), the wise official will walk them through the previous two steps and may refuse to bring the allegation to committee or intervene until that person has talked directly to the pastor. The exception to this rule is when the party has been accused of sexual misconduct, sexual abuse, financial impropriety, illegal acts or other unethical behavior. In these cases, the official body or supervisor must act with due diligence and appropriate confidentiality. These exceptions, however, prove the rule that church councils and official boards should only intervene in situations where the offended party has exhausted all avenues of direct confrontation.

4) If the church council or other official committee is unable to convince the offender to change his or her behavior, Jesus then allows that the church may treat the person as if he or she is "a Gentile and a tax collector" (Matthew 18: 17). This is remarkable language when one considers how Jesus received the irreligious and tax collectors of his day. The church has the power to remove a person who misbehaves from church leadership, but they should not write the person off in terms of loving outreach. I recently was involved with a council that acted to bar a disruptive individual from church office for a period of two years. They made it clear to him that he was

still welcome in worship and would be always in their hearts
and prayers.

5) Jesus concludes his teaching on conflict resolution by
reminding his followers that the way the church treats difficult individuals may have eternal consequences for that
person. Jesus says, "Truly I tell you, whatever you bind on
earth will be bound in heaven, and whatever you loose on
earth will be loosed in heaven" (Matthew 18:18). Jesus
speaks here of both awesome authority and overwhelming
responsibility. Could it be that the persons we cut off from
the grace of Christian fellowship in the course of a conflict
will be lost from the kingdom? Whatever our theology, this
passage should give us pause. Instead of blithely engaging in
what feels good to us in the midst of a conflict, we should be
carefully following the above process. Further, we should do
all that is in our power to make the church a place of healing
and compassion.

Preventive Maintenance

The conflict-resolution process that Jesus presents in Matthew 18 is
not meant to be the tool of last resort. I did not tuck it away on this last
page with that in mind. Instead, I hope you will notice how it summa-
rizes the key themes of this book. Church conflict is not an isolated
event that we can address without considering how the entire congregation behaves as a system. Correcting a congregation's system or culture
requires education and often the implementation of a step-by-step procedure. When Jesus tells us how to handle interpersonal conflict, his
teaching delineates a witnessing role for fellow Christians to play, as well
as authorizes church-council and denominational authorities to act as
final arbiters. One should never attempt to solve church conflict in iso-
lation. Each incident is part of a larger narrative of congregational
history. Each issue relates to the whole style of organization and decision-making that has become customary for that fellowship.

Jesus assumes that effective church leaders will teach and model this conflict tool, as well as his other teachings about loving relationships. Every church leader, clergy and lay, has a responsibility to care for the whole system of the local church. If people do not know how to get along, then they must learn better relationship skills. If miscommunication and gossip in the church hurts people, then leaders must find a better means for spreading information. Conflict is not an evil in itself. Rather, it is a wake-up alarm reminding us of further work we need to do.

With this in mind, I want to conclude as I began by repeating that we should never attribute to malevolence that which is merely due to incompetence. Few church leaders take the time to study conflict. The church has, in general, failed to implement Jesus' teaching on interpersonal relationships. All of us have been more willing to blame individuals for problems in the church rather than exploring the deeper systemic causes. Prayer, study, and participation in a small group that holds us accountable for our spiritual growth can be of infinite help. Don't look at whatever troubles may have caused you to read this book as isolated problems that you need to solve and forget. Instead, seek to learn from them and to expect other challenges. Grow each day in grace and wisdom as a Christ-like and compassionate leader.

I close with this New Testament prayer:

> Now may the Lord of peace himself give you peace at all times in all ways. The Lord be with all of you (2 Thessalonians 3:16).

Other Books by Bill Kemp

Each of the six books in the Congregational Leadership Empowered for Change series will focus on problems that can become woven into a congregation's very culture and so need the coordinated work of many people to achieve change. The emphasis is upon cultivating a broad leadership base that is aware of the issues and of implementing systemic changes. These books provide a common language that laity and clergy can use together when they talk about the things that influence the success of their congregation.

- *Ezekiel's Bones* reveals how spiritual passion is the fuel that keeps a congregation active and excited about the faith it has to share with the world. Without spiritual passion, a church, no matter its size, will either crash and burn or become a hollow shell of its former glory. Just as the body is fueled by a nutritious diet, so a church is fueled by a healthy, passionate spirituality.

- *Peter's Boat* looks at a common condition in today's world: burnout. Burnout threatens our relationships and our ability to function, especially as disciples of Jesus Christ. For everyone in the church, this book identifies the factors that lead to burnout and offers solutions to perfectionism, negative self-image, work addiction, and overload.

- *Jonah's Whale* discusses how to keep the congregation united behind a common vision. How do we get to where we are going unless we know where it is and what path we should take towards it?

- *Saul's Armor* looks at facility issues as well as the problem of creating a flexible and dynamic committee structure in your church so that your administrative process supports (rather than hinders) programs.

- *David's Harp* deals with preventing, managing, and transitioning out of conflict. Every pilot must communicate and respond to negative information in order to avoid stormy weather and collisions with other planes. We tend to treat conflict as an unwelcome intruder, rather than a routine part of flying. This book helps church leaders not to panic, but to see God's purposes in stressful situations.

- *Jesus' New Command* deals with how to unite the congregation into a strong faith community. Love is like oxygen, vital to the maintenance of church life. This book provides tools for building intimate small groups while encouraging the congregation to be welcoming to newcomers.

Holy Places, Small Spaces (Discipleship Resources, 2005) looks at how small-church fellowships are faring compared to other congregations. It addresses the critical clergy-supply problem and charts the changes that must take place for there to be a hopeful future of survival and growth for these congregations.

The Church Transition Workbook (Discipleship Resources, 2004) describes a step-by-step process that will enable the church to get moving again after traumatic conflict or being "run over by change." It keeps laity and clergy on the same page, as the church redefines pastoral relationships. The book includes stories, practical tools, and activities that will help the church see its current reality and the possibilities for ministry.